Computers and Communications

Computers and Communications
A Vision of C&C

Koji Kobayashi

The MIT Press
Cambridge, Massachusetts
London, England

Second printing, 1988

This translation © 1986 by the Massachusetts Institute of Technology
Originally published in Japan by The Simul Press, Inc., Tokyo, under the
title *C&C Modern Communications: Development of Global Information Media*
Copyright © 1985 by Koji Kobayashi

This book was set in Baskerville by The MIT Press Computergraphics
Department and printed and bound by Halliday Lithograph in the
United States of America.

Library of Congress Cataloging-in-Publication Data

Kobayashi, Koji, 1907–
    Computers and Communications: a vision of C&C
    Bibliography: p.
    1. Digital communications. 2. Computer networks.
I. Title.
TK5103.7.K6313   1986   384.3   85–24144
ISBN 0–262–11111–X

To scientists and engineers worldwide
who have contributed to C&C

Contents

Foreword

This book is simultaneously a biography of a successful telecommunications company and an autobiography of an outstanding and important figure in contemporary computer communications. It combines a description of contemporary information technology and its history with a vision of its role in societal evolution, past and projected. The author, Dr. Koji Kobayashi, believes, as I do, that the marriage of passive communications systems and the computer as a processor and manipulator of information has created a new discipline, one that he calls C&C (computers and communications) and one I think of as the information sciences, a discipline that is changing the basic character of society and vastly expanding human creative capabilities.

Dr. Kobayashi tells his story as the biography of NEC, the company he directs, formerly known as Nippon Electric Co., Ltd. His focus provides the reader with insights into how this most successful of high-technology companies was born, how it grew, how it competes with its national siblings, and how it has prospered by keeping itself at the leading edge of technology. It also explains how NEC's objectives are related to the imaginative national goal of the Japanese.

The success of NEC demonstrates that behind every great company there is an outstanding leader. Leadership is a mysterious talent, an amalgam of vision, energy, understanding of institutional goals and purposes, knowledge of the substance of the basic work involved, and a genuine concern for human beings. The nature of its role becomes evident in a comparison of mature American and Japanese firms. Their essential difference lies in the divergence between the philosophies expressed by the terms "good management" and "great leadership." American firms are built by visionary technical leaders, but as they grow and prosper they tend to fall under the spell of people whose major emphasis is good management. Even very large Japanese firms tend to retain leadership that places an emphasis on the technical aspects of the business. One component of Dr. Kobayashi's style, which emerges clearly in the narration, is his thorough understanding of the technical aspects of the fields in which his company operates.

Nippon Electric Company, as Dr. Kobayashi explains in his book, was founded eighty-six years ago as a joint venture of AT&T's subsidiary, Western Electric, and Japanese investors. This arrangement gave Nippon Electric Company unique access to Western Electric Company products, the Bell Telephone Company research and researchers, and, perhaps most important of all, to the example set by the Bell System's style of operations and commitment to high-quality performance. The formal collaboration between the two groups ended in the 1930s, when the U.S. Department of Justice forced AT&T to divest itself of its international communications operations. The AT&T stake in overseas telephone and manufacturing operations, including that in Nippon Electric Company, was taken over by International Telephone and Telegraph, but informal relationships continued between many individuals at Nippon Electric Company and the Bell Telephone Laboratories. Following World War II, many of these relationships were renewed and new ones formed. It was through these associations that Dr. Kobayashi came to visit MIT and I came to know him and NEC.

Dr. Kobayashi, as he says, had early become convinced that the fields of computation and communication would ultimately merge and that the techniques of information processing would profoundly alter the nature of communication systems. Consequently he found the research in these fields at MIT particularly interesting. We, likewise, resonated to his concepts of C&C and learned from each other about what has come to be known as the knowledge industry. More than half of his book is devoted to the questions and problems of this new industry: problems posed by the design of new equipment and of special software, by the development of human-machine interfaces and increasingly higher-level languages, and ultimately by the facilitation of communications between individuals everywhere by real-time machine translation of language.

Dr. Kobayashi describes in great detail how he expects innovations in C&C to affect society's enterprises. His division of that impact into vertical layers ranging from the smallest units in the home and office to global networks provides a useful framework for understanding how the new technologies will affect the ways people live, work, and interact. His is perhaps the clearest presentation I have read of what is meant in Japan by "the communication society" and also the goals of the collaborative industrial effort to create what is known as "the fifth generation computer." The former visualizes making the full power of modern information technologies available to the entire society. The latter can best be described as an integrated family of high-performance machines and software developed to accomplish the many tasks in which Dr. Kobayashi and others expect that machines will complement human efforts.

The ideas that form the technological basis of these ambitious plans come from everywhere, but especially from the United States. The Japanese contribution to the evolution of a worldwide information society is an understanding of its full potential and a willingness to undertake the long-term development efforts required to make it a reality. If American and European companies want to have a part in this development, they will have to enter the dream and match their efforts to it.

The vision that underlies Dr. Kobayashi's account is one of great power and hope. It articulates a future in which individuals everywhere can communicate with each other, in which knowledge is universally available and C&C information systems overcome not only barriers of distance but barriers of language, leading inevitably to a single, coherent, and competitive but friendly world. We can all look forward to its realization and all hope that it quickly becomes reality.

Jerome B. Wiesner

Preface

As an employee and later chairman of the board and chief executive officer of the NEC Corporation, I have been involved in communications equipment, electron devices, and more recently computer businesses for the past fifty-six years.

The NEC Corporation originated in 1899 as the Nippon Electric Company, Limited, through a joint venture between Japanese investors and the Western Electric Company, Incorporated (a subsidiary of the American Telephone and Telegraph Company), to produce telecommunications equipment in Japan. It is said to be the very first joint-venture company in Japan. At the time of its inception the company employed just 100 people; it manufactured magneto telephone sets as well as telephone switchboards which it supplied to Japan's Ministry of Communications. In 1925 the shares owned by Western Electric were transferred to the International Telephone and Telegraph Corporation (ITT) in the United States.

I joined NEC as an engineer in 1929 right after graduating from the Electrical Engineering Department of Tokyo Imperial University. At that time NEC had about 1,600 employees. This was at the beginning of the worldwide economic depression, and eventually about one-third of these employees had no work to do. It was during this period that ITT decided to transfer the management control of NEC to the Sumitomo Limited Partnership in Japan. Thus NEC came under Japanese management control for the first time, thirty-three years after its foundation.

(NEC became an independent company after World War II when big financial groups called *zaibatsu* were dissolved by order of the Allied occupation forces headquarters.)

Under such circumstances the company's employees felt they had to think up projects to make work for themselves. It was then that I began considering how the company might develop electric power line carrier telephone equipment competitive with U.S. and German equipment then on the market. At that time virtually one company in the United States and one company in Germany were the leading manufacturers of this type of equipment, which was based on electric power technology. However, my colleagues and I decided to develop the equipment using telecommunications technology. We were successful, and our equipment was adopted by electric power companies in Japan and also by the Korean Hydroelectric Power Company. This electric power line carrier equipment was widely used in this region by electric power companies until the advent of microwave communications systems after World War II.

At that time Japanese economic activities in former Manchuria (now the northeastern part of the People's Republic of China) were rapidly developing and a number of Japanese were immigrating to the area. Therefore the demand for communications between Japan and former Manchuria was on the rise. Only a shortwave radio communication system was capable of covering the long distance involved. But the shortwave radio was not satisfactory because of a signal fading problem, so Japan's Ministry of Communications was very interested in developing a telecommunications system utilizing cable circuits.

The prevailing method then for reducing transmission loss in cable circuits was to insert loading coils at regular intervals, a method invented in 1900 by Michael I. Pupin of Columbia University in New York. However, both frequency bandwidth and transmission distance were restricted due to delay distortion. So it was felt that cable circuits using loading coils were not suitable for this project, which involved a distance by cable of more than 3,000 kilometers. This problem was resolved by Shigeyoshi Matsumae and Noboru Shinohara, engineers at the

Ministry of Communications, who proposed a revolutionary nonloaded cable carrier system in which cable loss was compensated by amplifiers, eliminating loading coils.

As a representative of NEC, I participated in the project to develop and manufacture a nonloaded cable carrier system to link Tokyo and Mukden (now Shenyang), located in former Manchuria, a distance of 3,000 kilometers. This project was completed in 1939.

The period just after the Second World War was a time of rehabilitation for Japan's communications industry. It was then as general manager of the Tamagawa plant that I advised the top management of NEC to place greater emphasis on technological development. This was because I believed that communications should not be restricted by national boundaries but should have a larger mission of connecting remote parts of the world. I also foresaw how this would lead to the creation of new markets. After starting with microwave communication systems, development progressed to troposcatter communication systems and satellite communication systems. Experience has confirmed my belief that communications transcends national borders.

As microwave systems developed, television broadcasting networks expanded. I recognized that the contents of communications were greatly expanding as well—from telegraph and telephone messages to data, video, and graphics.

The company had become involved in computers in the mid-1950s at the beginning of their development, starting with small- and medium-scale computers and moving to large-scale computers and then from off-line to on-line computers in accordance with market requirements. With the advent of transistors, NEC also became actively engaged in developing processes to manufacture these revolutionary devices. As transistors gave way to integrated circuits (ICs) and large-scale integrated circuits (LSIs), and as communications systems became digitalized, I speculated that computers would someday be an integral part of communications networks and envisaged the concept of integrating computers and communications, which I call C&C.

I presented this concept in 1977 at INTELCOM 77 (the International Telecommunication Exposition) held in Atlanta, Georgia [1], and in 1978 at the Third U.S.-Japan Computer Conference, held in San Francisco, California, where I was a keynote speaker [2]. I stressed then that computers would develop to distributed processing and that total communications systems, including switching and transmission, would follow digitalization.

I later addressed the 23rd IEEE Computer Society International Conference held in Washington, D.C., in 1981, where I elaborated on the concept of "Man and C&C," describing how human interaction can be considered in the development of software [3]. In 1982, at the IIC (the International Institute of Communications) Annual Conference held in Helsinki, Finland, I first presented my ideas on how C&C could be extended to broadcasting [4].

In the following year—six years after I coined the term C&C in Atlanta—I spoke before FORUM 83 (the 4th World Telecommunication Forum) held in Geneva, Switzerland, under the auspices of the International Telecommunication Union. There I presented a full picture of C&C's position in the modern communications age, that is, toward the twenty-first century [5].

In this book I have brought together these published papers, added new chapters, and compiled them. This book has been written from the standpoint of the experiences and perspectives of an engineer turned chief executive, rather than in a scholarly and systematic style.

Writing this book would not have been possible without the helpful assistance of many people. Especially, Drs. Yukimatsu Takeda, Kiichi Fujino, and Nobuhiko Shimasaki provided invaluable assistance in the compilation and editing of the text. I would also like to say a special thank you to the many people who were involved in the preparation of the English text, notably Masateru Takagi, Yasukuni Kotaka, Kiyoshi Emi, Terence Esmay, and Mayuri Endoh, operator of the NEC APC III personal computer.

Computers and Communications

1

Pioneering Events in Communications Technology in Japan

In 1937 I had the opportunity to visit the United States for the first time. During a tour of the facilities of the Bell Telephone Company, I was greatly impressed by the confident prediction of a female supervisor: "We are aiming to be able to make connections with any place in the United States within three minutes."

In 1954, when I revisited the United States, I asked people I met, "What has contributed most greatly to the rapid realization of the wonderful modern civilization in this country?" The majority replied, "The development of communications and transportation." This too made a strong impression on me.

In Japan before World War II the development of telecommunications was far behind the United States. For example, it took just about a full day before you could talk after applying for a long-distance telephone call between Tokyo and Osaka, a distance of about 500 kilometers.

What was the reason for this situation? Was it due to a lag in telecommunications technology in Japan, or was it due to the way in which the telecommunications business was run? I believe that it was the latter.

From the start the Japanese telecommunications business was operated by the government, which controlled exclusively the use of radio waves. Technological development may have been sporadic and unsystematic, but in some instances the forerunners of the present communications technology can be seen.

After World War II, first the use of radio waves was released by the enactment of the Radio Waves Laws, and then the telecommunications business was transferred to a semigovernmental corporation by the inauguration of the Nippon Telegraph and Telephone Public Corporation. This allowed full-scale development finally to begin.

Some Early Representative Successes and NEC

Wireless Dispatches by the S.S. Shinanomaru

The role of wireless dispatches by the Japanese patrol ship S.S. *Shinanomaru*, in successfully communicating the movements of the Russian Baltic fleet just before the battle at the Sea of Japan in 1905, is remembered to the present day.

The apparatus used is believed to be spark-type wireless telegraph equipment developed by Matsunosuke Matsushiro, an engineer at the Electro-Technical Laboratory of the Ministry of Communications. This was just four years after the successful experiment of the transatlantic wireless telegraph transmission by Marconi in 1901. Matsushiro later joined NEC and participated in its management.

Invention of the TYK-Type Wireless Telephone

Taking the story out of sequence a bit, the first major project I became involved in after joining NEC was the development of electric power line carrier telephone equipment.

Later I learned that the fundamental principles for this carrier telephone were also invented and patented in Japan, quite independent of similar equipment developed by Western Electric. This was the product of research and a series of inventions by three engineers, Uichi Torikata, Eitaro Yokoyama, and Masajiro Kitamura of the Electro-Technical Laboratory of the Ministry of Communications: the TYK-type wireless telephone in 1912, the high-frequency telegraph and telephone in 1918, and the electric power line carrier telephone in 1919.

First Export of Telephone Office Equipment to China

In the early 1910s all telegraph and telephone businesses in China were under the control of Euro-American enterprises. This situation prompted the Chinese government to try to operate the telegraph and telephone business directly. As a start it purchased the Hankow Telephone Company in 1915. The government then planned to expand the Hankow telephone office and to construct another telephone office in Wuchang, with toll telephone circuits connecting the two places. A policy of calling international bids for the project was established. A Japanese group submitted an offer through the Sino-Japanese Industry Company, a joint-venture firm representing the Chinese government and Japanese business circles, and succeeded in winning the bid.

One stipulation was that all the equipment and materials necessary for the project must be procured from Japan. For this purpose several auxiliary equipment and materials manufacturers, and mainly NEC, cooperated to meet these requirements, though with aggressive guidance and support by Japan's Ministry of Communications. The installation work can be considered either a matter of victory or defeat for the project in that it was not possible to test the entire system before it was shipped from Japan. The equipment made by NEC was sent directly to the site, and it was assembled and installed there.

Fortunately both installations were completed smoothly, the Hankow telephone office of 2,200 lines in May 1917 and the Wuchang telephone office of 1,100 lines in February of the following year. The Japanese group's effort surprised and greatly pleased the Chinese government.

The excellent results obtained in this project proved that the products manufactured by NEC and other makers in Japan could compare favorably with those produced in Europe or the United States. At the same time the project prompted a remarkable development in Sino-Japanese economic cooperation.

Development of Proprietary Technologies

The Start of Radio Broadcasting

In 1923 the great Kanto earthquake struck the Tokyo area, and downtown Tokyo was burned to the ground. The destruction of telephone lines caused major damage to the country's telecommunication network and led to widespread confusion and anxiety. This made the government recognize the importance of equipping the country with modern communications facilities, and two major policies were decided on that led to the establishment of radio broadcasting stations and the adoption of an automatic telephone exchange system.

Medium-wave radio broadcasting began in 1925 with the establishment of the Japan Broadcasting Corporation (Nippon Hoso Kyokai in Japanese, abbreviated as NHK, which today is mainly maintained by subscribers). NEC supplied the broadcasting equipment which at first it imported from Western Electric. Later NEC decided to produce its own broadcasting equipment and then even proceeded to manufacture transmitting vacuum tubes.

In the 1930s, when Japan established a close economic relationship with northeastern China, NEC was asked to produce high-power broadcasting equipment of 100 kilowatts for the Manchuria Telegraph and Telephone Company, which it delivered in 1937. Also the 120-kilowatt high-power transmitting tube used for the equipment was developed and manufactured by NEC. Both products set records for output power among Japanese products at that time.

The Domestic Production of Automatic Telephone Exchange Equipment

The automatic telephone exchange systems in Japan began in the Tokyo area as part of a program to rehabilitate the capital from the disastrous earthquake of 1923. As the government gradually began to install the systems developed in Europe and the United States, it found inadequacies. It turned to NEC and other Japanese communication equipment makers to improve the imported systems. The Japanese communication equipment makers responded aggressively, and eventually automatic telephone exchange systems began to be manufactured domestically.

The domestic manufacture of telephone exchanges provided the momentum for Japan to undertake independent technological development in all types of communications.

Invention of Photograph Transmission Equipment

Spurred by the prevailing emphasis on independent technological development, NEC began next the development of photograph transmission equipment, which is the basis of today's facsimile equipment.

In 1928 the coronation of the present emperor, Hirohito, was scheduled to take place in Kyoto. All newspaper companies planned to transmit the pictures taken at the ceremony from Kyoto to Tokyo by telephone wire. To accomplish this, most newspapers expected to import foreign equipment. NEC, however, attempted to develop its own system, under the direction of Yasujiro Niwa, chief engineer, and Masatsugu Kobayashi, engineer. It met the challenge splendidly, and a newspaper company quickly adopted NEC's telephotographic system. On coronation day only the NEC system was able to provide prompt photo coverage of the ceremony to readers in the Tokyo area.

Later, in 1936, experiments in transmitting wireless photographs between Tokyo and Berlin, Tokyo and London, and Tokyo and San Francisco were successful. At that time the Olympic Games were being held in Berlin, and pictures showing exploits of Japanese athletes were continuously transmitted to Japan to the great excitement of the public.

The innovations in this technology continued after World War II. The field received a major impetus in the early 1970s when in 1972 the Japanese government released its control of communications circuits. Rapid growth of facsimile equipment followed.

Photograph transmission equipment developed by NEC in 1928

For his seminal achievement and subsequent contribution to facsimile transmission technology, Yasujiro Niwa was awarded the Japan Academy award in 1937 and the Order of Cultural Merits in 1957.

Development of the Remote Supervisory Control System

NEC also became involved in a series of research projects on remote supervisory control systems. The research was begun in 1928 through the entirely independent initiative of Yasujiro Shimazu, an engineer with the company. In the 1930s the system progressed from the code type to the synchronous type and then to the two-stage synchronous selective type, with which an extremely reliable system was realized. In Japan this system was first adopted by the electric power companies and the railways, enabling unattended operation of power plants, substations, and switching stations owned by electric power and railway companies.

The components used in the first stage of development were mainly rotary switches and relays. After World War II remarkable progress was made in the performance of control systems as these components were replaced by vacuum tubes, then by transistors, and finally by integrated circuits (ICs). With these technological advances use of control systems expanded, from electric power to communications, railway signaling, and broadcasting. Indeed, although often unrecognized, the remote supervisory control system has become an extremely important basic technology, allowing unattended operation of relay stations and transmitting stations, as well as facilitating maintenance.

The Challenge: Developing New Technologies

Development of the Nonloaded Cable Carrier Telephone System

Along with the progress made in refining existing technologies to promote domestic technological development, some companies chose to develop new technologies to meet new demands as well as new markets.

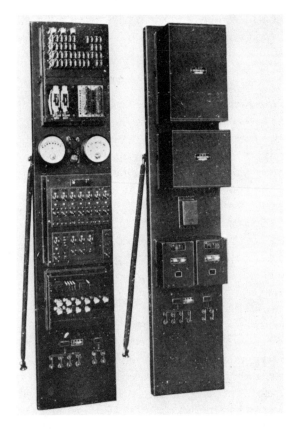

Remote supervisory control system developed by NEC in 1928

The development of the nonloaded cable carrier telephone system, which was proposed by Shigeyoshi Matsumae and Noboru Shinohara, engineers of the Ministry of Communications, is a case in point.

The distance between Tokyo and Mukden (now Shenyang), a central city in former Manchuria (now the northeastern part of the People's Republic of China), is about 3,000 kilometers by cable. At that time the shortwave radio was the only means of long-distance telephone communication. However, fluctuations in radio wave propagation made it a very unreliable medium. The only satisfactory alternative, which would ensure signal stability as well as greatly increase communications volume, was to use long-distance cable circuits.

An inherent problem with cable circuits, however, is that electrical signals attenuate in proportion to cable length. To reduce such attenuation, the then standard approach was to load the cables according to the method invented by Pupin in 1900 which called for coils to be inserted at appropriate intervals. But the drawback of this loading method was that the transmittable frequency bandwidth was extremely restricted, so that only one telephone channel could be provided.

There were two basic ways of dealing with this problem. The solution widely adopted in Europe involved an elaborate scheme—known as the super lightly loaded method—whereby the loading would be decreased by increasing the number of telephone channels, though there still would be some increase in attenuation. The solution the Japanese chose to pursue was not to use the loading coils, which would restrict the transmission bandwidth and the number of channels, but rather to compensate for the attenuation of volume by using high-gain vacuum tube amplifiers.

This proved to be theoretically the correct choice. But we had to make two important improvements in the existing technology before we could proceed with the installation of the cable circuits. One was to develop the necessary stable high-gain, low-distortion repeater amplifier. The other was to reduce

Map of Japan and neighboring countries

the crosstalk likely to occur in cable circuits. A complicating factor was that the policy of the Ministry of Communications forbade the use of foreign patents.

The research for this national project started in 1932 and ended in 1939 with the completion of six-channel long-distance nonloaded cable carrier telephone circuits between Tokyo and Mukden. I was selected to be a member of the group from NEC whose objective was to develop the repeater amplifiers and terminal equipment. And fortunately, with the assistance of Yujiro Degawa and Takeo Kurokawa, we could achieve this

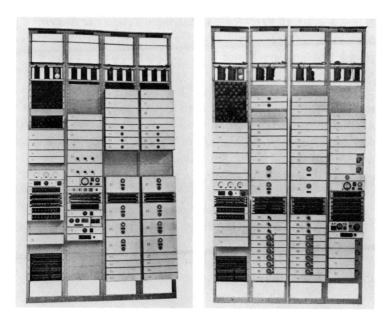

Nonloaded cable carrier telephone system developed by NEC in 1939

goal. As for the problem of crosstalk, the domestic cable manufacturers involved in the project successfully developed a new type of product with the signal transmission characteristics specified by the Ministry of Communications.

The cables were laid over the entire route of 3,000 kilometers, starting at Tokyo, running west through Japan's main island (Honshu) to Fukuoka, crossing the Korean strait by submarine cable, running north to Sinuiju on the Korean peninsula, crossing the Yalu River, and reaching Mukden via Dandong and Fengcheng. At that time it was without precedent; it was one of the world's longest telephone cable lines.

Development of VHF Radio Multiplex Telephone System

Soon after the development of the nonloaded cable carrier telephone system, the Ministry of Communications proposed a VHF radio multiplex telephone system.

This system would span the Tsugaru Strait, in order to surmount a communications bottleneck between Hokkaido, Japan's northernmost major island, and the main island. This project proceeded under the direction of Shigeru Yonezawa, engineer of the Ministry of Communications. NEC was chosen for the project because of its experience in research on frequency division modulation multiplex systems. NEC also submitted a proposal for a rectified negative feedback modulation method. Nobutaka Tanaka was the head engineer of the NEC group assigned to the project.

A six-channel VHF radio multiplex telephone system across the Tsugaru Strait was completed in 1940. This is thought to be one of the world's earliest radio multiplex telephone systems.

Research on Television

Research on television in Japan was undertaken by several universities and laboratories in the 1930s shortly after its inception in the West. While the majority of these institutes used rotary disk-type receivers, Kenjiro Takayanagi of the Hamamatsu Higher Technical School began experimenting with the Braun tube (cathode-ray tube) for receiving images—the only person in Japan to do so, and his research was conducted independently of similar experimentation in the United States.

Today's Japanese television picture tubes are the direct descendants of Takayanagi's applications of the Braun-tube technology of that time, and his farsightedness in recognizing the vast potential of the CRT deserves special mention.

NEC also made great efforts to develop technologies related to television relay and broadcasting, aiming at covering the Olympic Games scheduled to be held in Tokyo in 1940. However, the Tokyo Olympic Games were canceled due to the Sino-Japanese incident, and later this research was interrupted by the outbreak of World War II.

Research on Switching Circuit Network Theory

At the beginning of the development of electrical communication technology in Japan, telephone exchange technology was still very outmoded. Telephone exchange equipment, however, continued to depend on mechanical relays and step-by-step switches. Remarkable progress was made in the carrier and radio communications fields with the introduction of vacuum tube circuits.

Research on switching circuit network theory, a unique field of study at that time, was begun at NEC by engineers Akira Nakashima and Masao Hanzawa. The first results of the research on the theory were presented in 1935, and other research projects followed [7].

Until that time there had been no theoretical method for designing switching circuit networks. Instead, the design depended mostly on the experience of the designer. Nakashima and Hanzawa established the basis of a theoretical design method for switching circuit networks by introducing an algebraic code of zero for switch-on, infinity for switch-off. They later found that this code agreed completely with the characteristics of propositional calculus created by the British mathematician George Boole in the mid-nineteenth century, which is known as Boolean algebra.

Regrettably Nakashima and Hanzawa could not present the results of their epoch-making research outside of Japan because of the turbulent world situation. In 1938, two years after they first made known their switching theory in Japan, C. E. Shannon of Bell Telephone Laboratories in the United States presented almost identical research results and gained widespead recognition for his achievement in the engineering community [8].

Over the years mechanical contact switches have given way to electronic switches such as semiconductor diodes, transistors, and ICs. The classical switching circuits of Nakashima and Hanzawa have evolved into today's digital circuits—the indispensable constituent elements of computers and communications technology. What is more, expressing this operating theory by Boolean algebra is now common electrical engineering practice.

As we witness the remarkable development of digital circuit technology, it is no exaggeration to say that the Nakashima-Hanzawa theory was an important forerunner of today's most advanced digital systems.

Jumping to the postwar period, the first Japanese computer was the relay-type ETL MARK I, developed in 1952 by the Electro-Technical Laboratory of the Ministry of International Trade and Industry. It was constructed under the supervision of Mochinori Goto, and according to Hidetoshi Takahashi, a professor at the University of Tokyo at that time, it was based on the design theory derived from the Nakashima-Hanzawa theory [9].

The MARK I was succeeded by the MARK II, and development continued with the transistor-type MARK III and IV computers. Of these the MARK IV was to play the pivotal role in triggering the growth of Japan's computer industry.

Basic Research at Universities

Thus far I have described the major contributions in communications technology as they related to actual applications by the communications industry. Some Japanese universities conducted basic research in the communications field as well, and especially noteworthy among the contributions of these institutions are the research activities at Tohoku University.

In the 1930s electrical engineering in Japan was divided into so-called power engineering and weak electrical engineering (the burgeoning field of today's electronics engineering), and power engineering prevailed. Tohoku University, however, established an Electrical Communication Research Laboratory to focus on the future of telecommunications, which was only a weak electrical engineering field. The laboratory concentrated on basic research, with impressive results. Here are some examples of its successes:

• Establishment of electro-acoustics and development of the vibrometer by Heiichi Nukiyama and Masatoshi Matsudaira.

- Invention of the guided wave antenna (known as the Yagi antenna) by Hidetsugu Yagi and Shintaro Uda.
- Research on VHF radio communication by Shintaro Uda.
- Invention of the split-anode-type magnetron by Kinjiro Okabe.
- Research and development of magnetic tape recording (high-frequency bias method) by Kenzo Nagai and Teiji Igarashi, an engineer at the Anritsu Electric Company—until that time magnetic recordings were made on wire, and quality was not satisfactory. With the success of this research, the tape-recording systems we use today became the standard.
- Research on semiconductors by Yasushi Watanabe—Watanabe was engaged in prewar research on electron emission mechanisms, namely mercury and oxide cathodes. This research is said to have served as the basis of the vigorous postwar research activities on semiconductor devices in Japan.

In the field of magnetic materials research, which of course is closely related to telecommunications, several remarkable inventions were made at Tohoku and other universities:

- The strong magnetic steels, such as KS steel and new KS steel, by Kotaro Honda and others of the Metal Materials Research Laboratory of Tohoku University.
- The high-frequency magnetic material, Sendust, by Hakaru Masumoto and Tatsuji Yamamoto of the same Metal Materials Research Laboratory.
- The strong magnetic steels, MK and MT steels, by Tokushichi Mishima and others of the University of Tokyo.
- The OP magnet and oxide core, as ferrite magnetic materials, by Yogoro Kato and Takeshi Takei of the Tokyo Institute of Technology.
- The invention of the R-cut quartz crystal oscillator having a zero temperature coefficient, by Isaac Koga of the University of Tokyo.

All these research-and-development activities have contributed greatly to the realization of the brilliant electronic technologies we take for granted today.

2

Challenges Facing Postwar Japan

Defeat came as a disastrous blow to Japan, and its people faced unprecedented, critical difficulties after the war. Yet under such severe circumstances two important reforms were wisely carried out in the communications field: the release of radio waves from government control and the inauguration of the Nippon Telegraph and Telephone Public Corporation.

The Release of Radio Waves

With the enactment and promulgation of the new Radio Waves Laws in 1950, radio waves, which were previously monopolized by the government, were made available for use by the private sector. Up to that time the use of radio waves was entirely under the control of the government, and commercial use was not permitted. What is more, only medium-wave radio broadcasting was conducted. With the enactment of the Radio Waves Laws, radio waves became essentially the property of the people, and through due procedures civilians became able to use them freely.

With radio broadcasting no longer monopolized by NHK, commercial broadcasting was started by many private companies. Broadcasting frequency was expanded from medium- to very-high-frequency band. Thus frequency modulation (FM) broadcasting also began.

Television broadcasting was started next, although for a while research on television technology that had begun before the war could not be resumed by order of the Allied occupation forces. But in 1951, when the peace treaty was signed, the ban was automatically lifted. NHK was first to begin television broadcasting, but soon many commercial television stations were formed. And as the technology progressed, programming changed from black and white to color.

NHK began telecasting using television broadcasting equipment made in the United States. NEC promptly proceeded to develop its own equipment, the first of which was delivered to the Chubu Nippon Broadcasting Company and the second to the Osaka Asahi Television Company. These are the first television broadcasting systems manufactured in Japan, and they functioned exceptionally well.

There is one thing in particular that I wish to point out. With the start of commercial and FM radio broadcasting and television broadcasting, a large market for radio and television receivers was naturally created. This boosted the domestic development and production of electrical household applicances, and advances in the electrical appliances industry later became an important motive force behind the development of the Japanese electronics industry, in which field it is now a world leader.

Clearly the release of radio waves was a pivotal event that set off a burst of activity that revitalized postwar Japan. In this sense it is quite significant that every year on the first day of June a grand "Radio Waves Day" celebration takes place to commemorate the promulgation of the Radio Waves Laws.

The Establishment of the Nippon Telegraph and Telephone Public Corporation

In 1952, two years after the government relinquished control of radio waves, the Nippon Telegraph and Telephone Public Corporation (NTT) was established, and control of the telephone business was transferred from the government to NTT. Thus the telephone system finally became public property—some sixty-three years after the Cabinet decided in 1889 that the system should be operated by the government.

NTT initiated a plan to construct a nationwide telephone network, with a twenty-year goal of eliminating the waiting time for telephone installation, in other words, immediate installation upon application by subscribers. In implementing the new plan, Takeshi Kajii, the first president of NTT, set forth a basic policy that "NTT should aggressively adopt all domestic and foreign technological advances for the rapid development of the telecommunications business in Japan." This goal was not achieved until 1977, twenty-five years later.

The expansion of the toll telephone network was started first. This telephone network could also be used to relay television signals between major cities in Japan and was needed for television broadcasting. NEC and other Japanese communications equipment firms could satisfy the requirements for a huge amount of communications equipment needed for the construction of the network.

The general public eagerly embraced the idea of having its own telephone network. Indeed, right after the war some talk of the idea of "farming village telephones" operated by the villages had been generated in rural areas, where the shortage of telephones was most acutely felt. This idea spread rapidly throughout the country. The establishment of NTT naturally met this perceived need for rural telephone systems.

NTT became a completely private firm in April 1985, and it changed its name to the Nippon Telegraph and Telephone Corporation, though it retained its shortened name NTT. It thus became the largest private company in Japan.

Reconstruction and the Quality Improvement Movement at NEC

When Japan was in utter turmoil after the war, NEC suffered profoundly. The company's accumulated experience and expertise as a communications equipment manufacturer in the forty-five years since its foundation were nearly lost, and the company essentially had to restart from square one.

NEC therefore set about rebuilding itself through a strategy of concentrating its efforts on the areas of strongest demand. NEC's activities in response to the release of radio waves and the founding of NTT were but one side of this aggressive approach. Early on NEC became involved in a move to improve the quality of all its products.

This effort coincided with the occupation policy at the time. In January 1946 the general headquarters (GHQ) of the Allied occupation forces requested that the communications equipment industry not only increase production volume but also improve the quality of their products in order to strengthen Japan's communications systems. Particularly, GHQ asked that the statistical quality control method advocated by Walter A. Shewhart of Bell Telephone Laboratories be applied to the manufacture of vacuum tubes.

NEC responded by immediately applying quality control to its vacuum tube manufacturing processes. This action was very successful, and the quality of NEC's vacuum tubes increased appreciably. This triggered other activities within the company for improving quality. Later GHQ gave strong encouragement and guidance for adopting quality control in all Japanese industries.

In 1950 W. E. Deming, a member of the drafting committee on wartime specifications related to quality control in the United States, came to Japan as a statistics consultant for GHQ. Taking advantage of this opportunity, the Union of Japanese Scientists and Engineers asked Deming to hold a series of special lectures on quality control. The impact of these lectures on the Japanese industrial world was immeasurable.

The royalties for the lecture proceedings were donated by Deming to the Union of Japanese Scientists and Engineers. In 1951 the Deming Prizes were established in honor of his achievements, with his donation generating the fund. Since then these prizes have been conferred annually to individuals or companies who have made outstanding achievements in quality control.

The Deming Prizes have played an important role in promoting and disseminating quality control activities in Japanese industries. NEC was awarded the Deming Application Prize in 1952 and the Japan Quality Control Medal in 1973. I myself have had the honor of being awarded the Deming Prize, in 1974, for contributing to the promulgation and development of quality control in Japan for many years.

In the beginning, quality control was limited to statistical quality control. It later progressed to total quality control (TQC), which includes control of production. This was further extended to the "ZD movement." ZD stands for "Zero Defects," originally a slogan advocated by Secretary of Defense Robert S. McNamara to the U.S. munitions industry. I became aware of this movement during a visit to the United States and promptly introduced it in NEC. This program was merged with TQC and further expanded.

Later the ZD movement was taken up by the Japan Management Association, and it became a kind of spiritual movement aimed at revolutionizing the attitudes of employees toward work in all Japanese industries. It may not be going too far to say that as a result of the success of this movement, the worldwide reputation that "made in Japan" is synonymous with "high quality" became established.

Further Improvement in Cable Carrier Transmission Systems

After the war the stranded wire-type nonloaded cable system developed domestically under the leadership of the Ministry of Communications continued to be improved. A sixty-channel multiplex system was put into service, though in the rest of the world the coaxial cable system was widely used. When NTT decided to proceed with both microwave circuits and coaxial cable circuits in parallel to achieve the rapid completion of nationwide toll networks, NEC was asked to supply both systems.

In analog-type frequency division multiplex systems, miniaturization of channel translating equipment was required for wide-band, multiplex operation. NEC concentrated on improving the filters, which were the essential part of the equipment. First, a new design theory of filters was established. Next, a high-performance ferrite for filter magnetic cores, called Ne-ferrite, was developed. With new filters and cores, NEC was able to succeed in achieving substantial equipment miniaturization. NEC also succeeded in developing smaller mechanical filters. These developments subsequently enabled super miniaturized equipment accommodating 240 channels per bay to be realized.

Next came the digitalization of carrier transmission equipment by pulse code modulation (PCM). NEC's research on digital communications began at its Central Research Laboratories with research on delta modulation. NEC succeeded in putting twenty-four-channel PCM carrier transmission equipment into practical use jointly with NTT in 1965. This was followed by a 400-megabit PCM system, one of the world's fastest, which was put into operation in 1966.

Advance into Microwave Communication Systems

New markets often demand new technologies. When the restrictions on radio waves were lifted, microwave communication technology was just starting to be developed by NEC. Requests for independent microwave communication networks poured in from the government, the Japanese National Railways, and electric power companies. NEC was able to seize the market by perfecting this new technology.

First, NEC started with the development of a 2,000-megaHertz pulse time modulation system. Tohoku Electric Company adopted the system, which was put into service in April 1953. This was the first unattended microwave relay route put into operation in Japan.

In 1950 the Ministry of Telecommunications decided to adopt the microwave communication system for nationwide telephone and television relay networks (later transferred to NTT). This project proceeded under the leadership of Shigeru Yonezawa, Koji Kurokawa, and Isao Someya of the Ministry.

NEC was asked to participate in the research and development of the system by the Electrical Communication Laboratory of the Ministry. NEC of course eagerly accepted this request and vigorously pursued a policy of developing and producing microwave communication systems as one of the company's main lines of business.

As a result, in April 1954, a 4,000-megaHertz 360-channel microwave relay route was opened between Tokyo, Nagoya, and Osaka, which incorporated traveling wave tubes for signal amplification. In conjunction with this, NEC amassed a great many technological innovations—among these, the invention of the single traveling wave tube oscillation and amplification combined system by Masasuke Morita and Masamichi Kenmoku and further transistorization of the equipment.

Microwave communication is global in nature. Therefore, from the beginning, NEC was determined not to limit its activities to the domestic market but to supply microwave equipment to countries around the world. The decision to pursue actively overseas markets was truly an appropriate one, as I look back on it now.

Starting with Southeast Asia, NEC has installed microwave communication systems in almost every part of the world, including Indonesia, Australia, India, Pakistan, Mexico, Brazil, Iran, and the United States. The microwave communication systems served as the prime mover for NEC's export activities.

As supplies of microwave communication systems proliferated, the task of effectively utilizing the limited radio frequency spectrum loomed large. To help solve this problem, digitalization was introduced in the microwave.

As mentioned previously, NEC had already on hand a considerable number of achievements in digital technology for cable carrier transmission systems. By integrating these basic technologies with those of the microwave, and introducing the multilevel phase modulation method, NEC succeeded in developing a 400-megabit high-speed digital microwave system. This system was later adopted by NTT.

In cooperation with NTT's Electrical Communication Laboratory, NEC also succeeded in experiments with an 800-megabit super high-speed system using millimeter wave guides, but this system was not put into use.

Development of the Troposcatter Microwave Communication System

Once NEC decided that its basic policy would be to seek markets for communications equipment all over the world, not just in Japan, it directed its strategies for developing technology appropriately. The troposcatter microwave communication system was one result of NEC's program to develop microwave communication systems for use throughout the world.

The phenomenon that microwaves are scattered in the troposphere, which is related to meteorological phenomena in the earth's upper atmosphere, was discovered by the Englishman E. Megaw around 1950. By utilizing scattered waves, the troposcatter system allows communication between remote locations on earth to proceed beyond the horizon. However, a high transmitting power of about 10 kilowatts is required, for the scattered waves are very weak. Therefore this system cannot be used for short-distance domestic communication because it will cause interference with other radio facilities.

In 1954 NEC succeeded in reducing the required transmitting power to one one-hundredth of conventional systems by adopting a high-sensitivity receiving system invented by Masasuke Morita and Sukehiro Ito. By reducing transmitting power, interference with other systems was reduced.

Thus high-sensitivity receiving systems have been used not only for over-the-horizon communications between Kyushu (Japan's southernmost major island) and Okinawa, and between outlying islands, but also for line-of-sight multiplex communications. Furthermore it has played a vital role in receiving systems for satellite communications.

3

In Search of New Communications Systems

Advance to Satellite Communications Systems

After the war I came up with the idea of laying a troposcatter-type microwave communication relay route between Japan and the North American continent, along the Kurile and Aleutian islands. NEC proceeded with its development.

Then, one day in July 1962, I was in Chicago and happened to switch on the television in my hotel room. And what should appear on the TV screen but a relay broadcast from Paris via the artificial satellite *Telstar 1*. I was very impressed by this achievement.

On my way back to Japan I stopped in Los Angeles to visit L. A. Hyland, vice-president of Hughes Aircraft. I learned there that an epoch-making idea for a synchronous satellite (also called geostationary satellite) had been proposed by H. A. Rosen, a young Hughes engineer, and that development was about to begin.

Unexpectedly, Hyland proposed that Hughes Aircraft and NEC jointly develop satellite communications technology. This was because he highly valued NEC's technical capabilities in microwave communications. I recognized the future importance of satellite communications and was convinced that this was the very field I had long been looking for the company to pursue.

NEC's journey into satellite communications thus began with the development of earth station receiving equipment. The first system was delivered to the Ibaraki Space Experimental Center of Kokusai Denshin Denwa Co., Ltd. (KDD, Japan's international telecommunications carrier), located northeast of Tokyo. On November 23, 1963, the first TV space relay experiments between the United States and Japan, which were initiated by Japan's Ministry of Posts and Telecommunications and KDD, were successfully conducted via *Relay* (medium-altitude) satellite, which was supplied by RCA. To mark this memorable event, a special message by President Kennedy was scheduled to be transmitted from the American station. However, the actual transmission was suddenly changed to the tragic news of the assassination of the president, which profoundly shocked and saddened us all.

Subsequently NEC supplied the complete systems for the Kashima Satellite Communication Earth Station of the Radio Research Laboratory, the Ministry of Posts and Telecommunications. In conjunction with the NASA's *Syncom 3* geostationary satellite, the station was used for transmitting TV coverage of the 1964 Tokyo Olympic Games throughout the world.

NEC and Hughes then jointly developed a demand assignment multiple access system for communications satellites and also conducted successful experiments on the ground to simulate satellite relay. This was named the STAR (*S*atellite *T*elecommunication with *A*utomatic *R*outing) system by Hughes. In 1965 NEC and Hughes invited J. V. Charyk, president of the Comsat Corporation, to Japan for a demonstration of ground simulation experiments with this system.

In 1966 Hughes and NEC jointly constructed a satellite communications experimentation center in Arkansas. Participants from the INTELSAT member countries in the satellite communication technology seminar held by the International Telecommunication Union were invited to this center for a demonstration of the STAR system, from which they gained a strong impression of the efficiency of the demand assignment multiple access system.

In 1965 the development of a new satellite communication system called SPADE commenced at Comsat under the direction of Charyk and S. Metzger. (SPADE stands for *S*ingle Channel per Carrier *P*CM Multiple *A*ccess *D*emand Assignment *E*quipment.) The system was successfully developed and has become the standard satellite communication system. Tadahiro Sekimoto, then an engineer and now the president of NEC, worked for Comsat as a researcher for about two years from August 1965, and later he participated directly in the development of the SPADE system as manager.

The basic technology of the SPADE system is pulse code modulation (PCM), which is a digital technology and one step ahead of the FM (frequency modulation) system used for the STAR system mentioned earlier. However, the basic system functions for SPADE were fostered by the STAR system.

NEC is indebted to the deep understanding and constant guidance of L. A. Hyland of Hughes and J. V. Charyk of Comsat during its development activities for satellite communication systems.

Advance into Optical Communication Field

Here I would like to take up one more important technological development—lasers and optical fiber cables for transmitting them. There are two types of laser generators: solid-state and gas. The former was invented by T. H. Maiman of Hughes Aircraft in 1960, and the latter by Ali Javan and others of Bell Telephone Laboratories in 1961.

From conversations with Hyland, I learned that the laser would soon be recognized as one of the greatest inventions of this century, with such great possibilities that it would quickly become very widely used. NEC promptly undertook the development of laser technologies, starting with experiments to transmit TV signals between plants in Kawasaki and Yokohama (about 11 kilometers) utilizing laser space propagation.

These experiments showed that there were various problems in stability with space propagation and that a line transmission system like the optical cable was preferable. Proposals for the transmission line included light beam guides and gas lens guided wave paths in the United States, and a graded index optical fiber in Japan, an idea proposed at Tohoku University. However, none of these systems was as yet realized.

Under these circumstances NEC and Nippon Sheet Glass Co., Ltd. jointly proceeded with research on optical fiber manufacturing methods using glass. In 1969 the companies succeeded in developing an optical glass fiber by a revolutionary method called the ion displacement process. This was called SELFOC (*Self-Foc*ussing glass fiber). Today it is used effectively for optical communication terminal equipment, medical equipment, and short-haul laser optical transmission.

In 1970 Izuo Hayashi, M. B. Panish, and others of Bell Telephone Laboratories succeeded in achieving continuous oscillation of double heterojunction semiconductor lasers at room temperature. Shortly thereafter NEC was also successful in similar experiments by Yasuo Nannichi (now a professor at the University of Tsukuba) at its Central Research Laboratories. Hayashi later joined NEC as a research leader in this field at its Central Research Laboratories.

As the development of low-loss long-distance optical cable progressed in the United States and Japan, NEC started to put optical communication systems into practical use by integrating these cables and equipment. As early as 1974 NEC succeeded in field trials of an optical communication system in cooperation with Tokyo Electric Power Company. This is considered to be one of the earliest applications of an optical communication system in the world.

In 1978 NEC delivered a system to the Vista-Florida Telephone System: this too is considered to be the first working optical communication system in the United States for commercial use. The SELFOC optical cable was adopted for this system.

In 1982 NEC delivered and installed digital optical communication networks connecting nine toll telephone offices in Buenos Aires, Argentina. At that time the optical fiber cable manufactured by Sumitomo Electric Industry Company, Ltd. was used, and the digital switching equipment was supplied by NEC. This was then one of the world's largest facilities using these new communications technologies.

NEC proceeded with advanced research on high-speed digital communication systems for optical fiber cables. The 560-megabit system that evolved from this research was displayed at TELECOM 83 which was held in Geneva, Switzerland. Next, NEC, in cooperation with the Electrical Communication Laboratory of NTT, succeeded in experiments on a 1.6-gigabit system.

Advance into the Semiconductor Device Business

Entering the Transistor Business

Not much has to be said about the invention of the transistor by Bell Telephone Laboratories in 1948—it was a truly revolutionary event. Jack A. Morton of the laboratories attributed this success to a large-scale systematic research effort directed specifically at developing such new active components as the transistor. Back in the late 1940s it was projected that by the year 2000 the volume of worldwide communications would be enormous and so would require extremely advanced telephone switching equipment. Vacuum tubes could not be used in more advanced systems because of their size and power consumption. Therefore it was necessary to find an entirely new component to replace the vacuum tube. Semiconductors (germanium and silicon) appeared promising because of their electrical conductivity properties. The researchers started with the study of these semiconductors. After ten years of research the transistor was finally invented by William Shockley, John M. Bardeen, and Walter H. Brattain.

The transistor, and later other semiconductor devices such as ICs, LSIs, and VLSIs (very large-scale integrated circuits), was to become the basic technology supporting the integration of communications and computer technologies. As you read this episode, you will understand that great expectations were placed on transistors.

However, at the very beginning there were questions about whether transistors could be practically applied or manufactured in large quantity at good yield. In fact at NEC there was serious hesitation about immediately beginning the mass production of transistors. NEC had already been manufacturing vacuum tubes, which since 1932 had been a major part of the company's business. Nevertheless, NEC was concerned that the new device might replace vacuum tubes, so the company immediately embarked on the development and trial manufacture of transistors.

Fortunately NEC had been involved in the research and development of the silicon diode as a mixing diode for the microwave, under the direction of Hiroe Osafune, and had the highest performing product on the domestic market. This served as a powerful springboard for a large-scale advance into the semiconductor device business.

NEC first decided to emphasize the development and production of semiconductor devices for communications equipment and industry use. In 1958 the company built Japan's first fully enclosed clean plant to be used exclusively for the manufacture of semiconductor devices. At NEC the semiconductor crystal material was changed from germanium to silicon at an early stage. In 1960 the company initiated research and development of integrated circuits. I remember that the cover of the July 27, 1962, issue of *Electronics* magazine published in the United States carried a picture of NEC's IC.

In 1967 NEC established its Integrated Circuits Division, the first such division in Japan, and prepared for full-scale manufacture of ICs. The company's semiconductor device business, which started from diodes and transistors, traced a steady course of development to ICs, LSIs, and VLSIs.

Cover of the July 27, 1962, issue of *Electronics* magazine

Digital technology is now a mainstay in modern telecommunications technology. It utilizes pulse code modulation (PCM), an epoch-making method invented in 1937 by A. H. Reeves of England. However, as that was the age of vacuum tubes, it was economically infeasible to put this technology into practical use, and it was left unutilized for a long time.

In 1962, a quarter century later, PCM was first put into service by Bell Telephone Laboratories in its twenty-four-channel carrier telephone equipment, named the T1 system. PCM equipment can be said to have been forced to wait until the advent of the transistor. This touched off the adoption of digitalization in all fields of communications technology.

Next, let us turn to the computer, which is also based on digital technology. The world's first electronic computing machine, ENIAC, was developed by the University of Pennsylvania in 1946 and used vacuum tubes—some 18,800 in all. Power consumption was 140 kilowatts, and total weight 30 tons—it was a real monster of a computer. In today's age of semiconductor ICs, such great progress has been realized that equipment with almost the same computation capability as ENIAC can be placed in the palm of the hand—the one-chip LSI electronic calculator.

Promotion of Transistorization of Communications Equipment

At NEC, as development and manufacture of transistors advanced, more and more of the company's communications equipment in all fields was becoming transistorized. Along the way the equipment people set severe requirements of performance, quality, and reliability for the semiconductor device people. Instead of this posing a problem, however, it was very impressive that both the equipment and the device people were able to stimulate each other so that development was accelerated. The one product area that was not transistorized was telephone switching equipment, whose major component consists of electromagnetic relays.

Japan's telephone switching business was monopolized by NTT, which had made a huge investment on a nationwide scale. Therefore it was very difficult to change the existing system, not only because of economic problems but also because of system technology problems. These are the problems we always face when applying revolutionary technologies to this field.

NTT reacted positively to the situation. In 1956 an Electronic Switching System Study project was inaugurated under the leadership of the Electrical Communication Laboratory. NEC also formally concluded a contract with NTT to participate in this study. In 1964 this developed into the New Switching Equipment DEX Study for Practical Use. This study led to the completion of the DEX-21 Electronic Switching System (analog type), which was put into service at NTT's Kasumigaseki Telephone Office in Tokyo in 1970.

Meanwhile, on its own, NEC began a trial transistorization of small-size private branch exchanges (PBX) in 1957. The first commercial 200-line Space Division Switching Equipment was completed in 1960 and delivered to Mitsukoshi Department Store in Nihonbashi, Tokyo. In the next year NEC produced an improved version of this equipment, which was supplied to the Shikoku Electric Power Company. Then, because the market was not favorable for further business development, the company was forced to wait until digital switching equipment could be exported to overseas markets.

Advance into the Computer Business

The Parametron Computer

As transistorization of communications equipment proceeded at NEC, improvements in performance and economy were steadily being realized. An especially important new technological feat further accelerated this trend. This was the birth of the electronic computing machine, which is now known as the computer.

The computer industry was started in Japan about ten years after it was developed in the United States. The world's first electronic computer, the ENIAC, was a huge vacuum-tube-type machine. In Japan two experimental vacuum-tube-type computers were manufactured.

The first was a computer designed and produced by Bunji Okazaki of Fuji Photo Film Co., Ltd. and was called FUJIC. It is said to have been completed in 1956 and used for lens design. This computer is now displayed at the Science Museum in Ueno Park, Tokyo, as the first computer made and practically applied in Japan. Mr. Okazaki later joined NEC and participated in the further development of computers.

The second computer was called TAC and was developed and manufactured for trial use by the University of Tokyo under the leadership of Hideo Yamashita, with the cooperation of Toshiba Corporation. Research began in 1952, and the equipment was completed in 1959. It was used for research activities at the university's Faculty of Engineering and related research laboratories.

At almost the same time a logic element named "parametron" was invented by Eiichi Gotoh, a graduate student of the Faculty of Science of the University of Tokyo, who later became a professor. Parametron is a kind of resonance circuit, consisting of a small magnetic core, coils, and capacitors, that applies the parametric excitation principle. It was slower in operation speed than transistors but was cheaper and just as stable.

To overcome the ten-year lag with the U.S. computer industry, NEC decided from the beginning to adopt both the transistor-type and parametron-type computers but to ignore the vacuum-tube-type completely.

Still, there was another motive for NEC's entering into the computer industry, related to the completion of a new design theory on wave filters at NEC. As mentioned earlier, NEC had for many years been engaged in the development and production of multiplex carrier transmission equipment. The parts that limited the performance of the equipment were the filters used for channel separation. The design methods for filters in use at that time, namely for Zobel (United States) and Cauer (Germany) filters, were based on the cut-and-try process.

Because NEC had been aggressively conducting research on filters, Hitoshi Watanabe conceived a new design theory in 1955 [11]. However, to apply the theory to an actual design effectively, it was essential that a number of numerical computations be conducted at high speed. But only mechanical calculators or punch card systems were available for such computation at that time. NEC engineers strongly felt computers that could perform large-scale scientific computations were needed and decided to develop a computer themselves by applying the parametron invented at the University of Tokyo.

NEC successfully manufactured its first trial computer in 1958. This was the NEAC-1101. This model led to the SENAC-1 (NEAC-1102,) which NEC developed jointly with Tohoku University. Next NEC completed an improved version, NEAC-1103, and supplied it to the Defense Agency Research Laboratory.

Based on these results, the company developed and mass-produced small-size computers for business use, the NEAC-1200 series, which were favorably received in the market. However, as it became apparent that parametrons could not compete with transistors in operation speed, NEC stopped further commercialization of parametron-type computers and moved promptly to transistor-type computers.

Conversion to the Transistor Computer

By the late 1950s years of research on computers, which started with the relay-type computer, were bearing fruit at the MITI's Electro-Technical Laboratory. The prototype of the transistorized computer ETL MARK IV was nearing completion under the direction of Hiroshi Wada, director of the electronics department of the laboratory.

NEC decided to introduce and commercialize this computer. This was the NEAC-2201, completed in 1957. At the recommendation of MITI, the first trial computer was displayed at the AUTOMATH (International Information Processing Conference) show held in June 1959 in Paris and was well received. This was thought to be the first transistor computer in the world to be marketed for the general public.

NEC further improved the NEAC-2201 by adding internal memory, external memory, and input and output equipment, thus taking it from the conventional simple calculator to a commercialized electronic data processing (EDP) system. This new computer, NEAC-2203, was introduced in 1959 and became widely used. About one year later transistor computers made in the United States appeared in the Japanese market.

In due course several Japanese makers entered this field, and imports from the United States increased. Thus the fledgling computer business became extremely competitive.

Exhibition of the first NEC transistor computer at AUTOMATH in Paris in 1959

Development of the On-Line System

At about the time NEC introduced the NEAC-2203 computer, the company was asked by Kinki Nippon Railways to develop a seat reservation system. This was the perfect opportunity for NEC to develop an on-line, real-time system. At that time non-error transmission technology for data to be transmitted on communication lines was being developed at NEC's carrier transmission division. The result was the first case of data transmission application.

By combining the technology of data transmission with that of the NEAC-2203 computer, NEC succeeded in developing Japan's first on-line seat reservation system, which was put into operation in 1960.

Development of the Time-Sharing System

The multiple access time-sharing system was gaining attention as the successor to the simple on-line system. The MAC system (or CTSS) and the more advanced MULTICS system developed by the Massachusetts Institute of Technology were the leading examples of this new system.

In 1959 NEC developed the NEAC-2202 which, although on a very small scale, could be shared by seven terminals based on the time division principle. This computer was first supplied to a securities company. In order to enter the field of large-scale time-sharing systems, NEC began to develop a system using MIT's MULTICS system as a model; Kyozo Nagamori, Hiroshi Kaneda, Yoshiteru Ishii, and Yukio Mizuno participated in the project. As a result the company succeeded in developing Japan's first time-sharing system in 1967, using NEC's large-scale computer NEAC-2200/500 as the main computer. It was named the MAC system, after a similar system at MIT, and was delivered to the University of Osaka where it was put into operation. With this, NEC's computer business evolved from medium-scale to large-scale systems and from off-line to on-line systems.

Development of Speech Recognition and Synthesis Technology

Trial Manufacture of Voice-Activated Typewriters

The basic medium of communication between human beings is, needless to say, the human voice. The pursuit of the substance of voices or speech may lead to the pursuit of the substance of communication.

With the rise of computers, it was expected that speech would someday become the ultimate interface between man and machine. Through research and development of speech bandwidth compression transmission equipment (VOCODER or Voice Coder), NEC was helping to deepen the understanding of the substance of speech.

In 1958 Toshiyuki Sakai of the University of Kyoto asked NEC to produce a research prototype of a speech typewriter as part of a joint research and development program. NEC

eagerly accepted this challenge and completed a trial manufacture of the typewriter in 1960. With this was realized the
first experimental equipment, which could recognize 100 mon-
osyllable, speaker-independent speech patterns in Japanese at
an accuracy of about 90 percent.

Based on this success, NEC vigorously undertook independent
research and development of speech recognition and synthesis.
The experience gained in these activities allowed NEC to understand fully the many difficulties that might lie ahead in this
field. In this sense the joint research and development project
with the University of Kyoto was an event worthy of special
mention for NEC.

Start of Full-Scale Research on Speech Recognition

On its own NEC started research on limited-vocabulary speech
recognition and later proceeded to research on connected-word
recognition. The research took about ten years, and the going
was not smooth.

Despite the difficulties, in 1969 NEC succeeded in developing
an epoch-making means for speech recognition, called the DP
matching method. This method enables a computer to analyze
and elucidate correctly speech patterns of words using a mathematical optimization method called dynamic programming (DP).
High-precision word recognition has become possible at last.
Subsequently, in 1974, NEC developed a more advanced, two-
level DP matching method that made recognition of continuously
voiced words possible. The results of these research activities
were presented in a paper delivered before the Institute of
Electrical and Electronics Engineers, Inc. (IEEE) [12]. Hiroaki
Sakoe, the author of the paper, received a Senior Award for
his paper by the Society of Acoustics, Speech and Signal Processing of IEEE in 1980. Around that time NEC manufactured
and supplied a trial prototype of voice-controlled package destination sorting equipment at the request of a manufacturer of
conveyors. The field test was extremely successful. In view of
these satisfactory results NEC made this system into a product

called DP-100 which was first marketed in 1978. This was among the very first commercial connected-word recognition equipment in the world.

All of the systems described here required preregistration of the voice of each user. Naturally NEC was not satisfied with such a limitation to its systems, so it immediately tackled the development of a more difficult speaker-independent system. As a result in 1980 NEC succeeded in putting such a system, named SR-1000, into production. This was promptly adopted by major banks in Japan as a new telephone banking system. The SR-1000 was also one of the very first such systems put into commercial service in the world.

We should not overlook the fact that the progress in research and development of speech recognition and synthesis systems would not have been possible without the continuous strides in development in semiconductor and IC devices and high-performance computers. NEC is vigorously continuing research and development in this field.

4

Toward C&C

Merging of Computer and Communications Technologies

In the late 1960s, as I saw that computers were progressing to on-line systems and that communications were gradually becoming digitalized, it appeared inevitable to me that the two would eventually be merged in the direction of information processing systems. However, before this merger could be realized, the focus of technology had to shift away from large-scale computers and also to make additional advances in the digitalization of telephone switching systems.

The first problem was gradually overcome with the development of smaller computer systems with remotely linked multiple terminals, which became known as "distributed processing systems."

In 1976 NEC introduced the distributed processing-type computer system "DINA," which incorporated NEC's knowledge and experience in communications technology. DINA stands for *D*istributed *I*nformation Processing *N*etwork *A*rchitecture. This computer system can be considered a natural development for NEC, a company that has been based on communications technologies since its foundation. This DINA system in turn helped to accelerate the digitalization of communications technology.

The second problem, the lag in digitalization of telephone switching systems, derived from the fact that many of the huge telephone networks already installed worldwide were based on analog technology. Japan's domestic telephone networks, whose operations were monopolized by NTT, were no exception. And of course manufacturers such as NEC were in no position to initiate changes in the system.

Because of the global nature of communications and the apparent limitations in the potential of development of the domestic market for communications networks, NEC began exploring overseas markets in the early 1960s.

In some countries, however, particularly the United States, Canada, France, and England, the move toward digitalization of telephone switching systems was beginning. Therefore NEC decided to enter the overseas digital switching system markets. In 1977 NEC introduced its first digital switching system for telephone offices, NEAX-61, at the INTELCOM 77 exposition held in Atlanta, Georgia [1]. With this achievement NEC now offered all the major systems required for digitalization of communications technologies.

Announcement of the C&C Concept

At INTELCOM 77 (International Telecommunication Symposium), government administrators, presidents of telecommunications companies, and top management of manufacturers who were engaged in the communications business from various countries around the world were present. I delivered the keynote address and found it a golden opportunity to air an idea I had nursed in my mind for years—my concept that computers and communications have been heading toward a merger since the introduction of semiconductor technology. This speech was received favorably, and many in the audience later told me they shared this feeling.

The following year at the Third U.S.-Japan Computer Conference held in San Francisco, California, I decided to expound on this concept. I presented my talk using the abbreviation "C&C" which stands for the integration of computers and com-

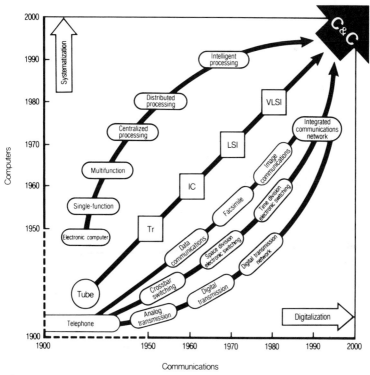

Figure 4.1
The general development of C&C

munications. I described my concept of C&C using the diagram shown in figure 4.1. Unlike my address at INTELCOM 77 in which I considered C&C mainly from the standpoint of communications technology, my presentation at the U.S.-Japan Computer Conference was mainly from the standpoint of computer technology. The keynote speaker from the United States was Jerome B. Wiesner, president of the Massachusetts Institute of Technology, who presented an insightful overview of information technology, from which I gained precious suggestions for the future.

C&C as Corporate Identity [13]

There was yet another motive that led me to pursue the C&C concept—the pursuit of what today is called "corporate identity." For some time I thought that the most important job for a top manager of a corporation is to chart unknown courses and to steer the good ship "Enterprise" as its captain. Shortly after I assumed the post of president at NEC in 1964, I read a book entitled *The Production and Distribution of Knowledge in the U.S.A.* written by Fritz Machlup of Princeton University. The important point I gleaned from the book regarding industrial activities was that we must rid ourselves of conventional materialistic and hardware-oriented ways of thinking and instead consider knowledge and information as essential to economic growth.

I later read an article, entitled "On the Information Industry," in a 1963 back issue of Japan's *Chuo Kohron* magazine which was written by Tadao Umezao of Osaka City University, who espoused a similar view. These men through their writings stirred in me an interest in the concept of a "knowledge industry." In 1965, when I was asked to speak before the Tokai Branch Meeting of the four major electrical engineering institutes held in Nagoya, Japan, I presented the concept of the knowledge industry as NEC's corporate identity theme.

I pursued this theme publicly again in 1966 when I was asked again to address the joint national convention of the four major electrical engineering institutes, this time held in Tokyo. On that opportunity I spoke on the perspective of "Japan's Knowledge Industry and the Standpoint of the Electronics Industry" based on various statistical data in Japan; at the heart of this, of course, was the future direction of NEC [14].

Indeed, "knowledge industry" represented the most appropriate theme for NEC. It was at this time that NEC decided to emphasize three main lines of business: communications, which transfer information; computers, which process information; and semiconductors, which serve as the basis of these technologies. Later, in the 1970s, as Japanese society became more information oriented, the concept of the knowledge industry became the subject of vigorous debate. The Japanese government in fact set out to place Japan's trade and industry policy on a knowledge-intensive course. As it turned out, the course I selected as a top manager of a private company later became the general trend of the Japanese industrial sector.

Developments Leading to C&C

Since I became president of NEC some twenty-one years ago, among the three separate fields I promoted, the advancement of semiconductor technology—from ICs to LSIs to VLSIs—was spectacular. Because I thought that this would surely lead to epoch-making changes in the fields of computers and communications, I decided to adopt C&C as NEC's new corporate identity. I saw the C&C concept as an extension of the knowledge industry concept I had established over a decade before.

As I look at the C&C concept now, I can consider broader, more global applications. First, clearly C&C represents the basic framework of the world's knowledge and information systems. Second, as the importance of knowledge and information, as new resources, increases worldwide, C&C will play an ever more central role in the development of economic activities and culture. Third, effective use of the earth's limited resources, such as energy and food, will become possible by efficient utilization of the knowledge and information available through C&C.

Another reason for my attraction to the concept of C&C is somewhat related to the concept of the Club of Rome's activities advocated in 1970 by the late Italian businessman Aurelio Peccei. I have participated in the activities of the Club as a member from the time of its establishment.

Returning to figure 4.1, at the lower right-hand side along the horizontal axis is shown the digitalization trend in communications. Telephone sets, facsimile equipment, telephone switching systems, and transmission systems were developed

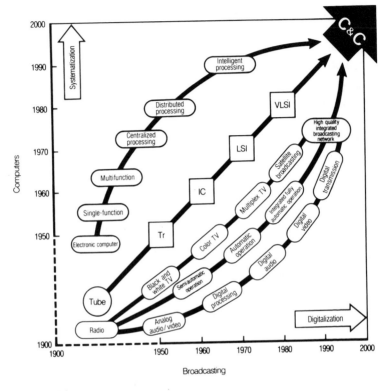

Figure 4.2
Development of C&C in broadcasting systems

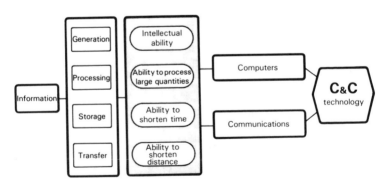

Figure 4.3
Expansion of human capabilities through C&C technology

separately, though all were based on analog technology initially. As digital technology is introduced, these products and systems are integrated into communication networks sharing digital technology. The International Telecommunication Union (ITU) has been engaged in standardizing the field via the integrated service digital network (ISDN).

The upper left half of the figure along the vertical axis traces the advancement of the digital computer. Over the years computers based on digital technology have developed from single-function to multifunction types, and to large-scale centralized processing. Then, with the introduction of digitalized communication technology, computers developed into distributed processing networks. Now the trend is toward intelligent processing. The progress in semiconductor components, which helped make the development of the computer possible both economically and technologically, is shown by the diagonal line.

Figure 4.2 shows the development of broadcasting systems, which has played an important role in communications. There are three areas that constitute broadcasting systems: radio and TV receiving systems, program transmission systems, and radio wave transmission systems. All three areas are changing from analog to digital systems, and broadcasting systems are moving toward high-quality integrated broadcasting networks.

Now let us consider the essential role of computer and communications technologies. As shown in figure 4.3, communications technology removes restrictions on distance and time in human information transfer capabilities. Computer technology removes limitations on quantity, time, and intelligence in its capacity to generate, process, and store information. C&C technology will enrich human life by completely integrating these two technologies. In fact I fully expect that a new culture based on C&C technology will emerge.

5

Background on the Development of Computers

There are two ways of looking at the development of computers. The first is to consider the great strides made in computer functions, that is, growth in intelligence; and the second is to look at the expansion of systematization capability from the standpoint of computer users.

In the first instance, computers have progressed from single-function to multifunction to centralized processing to distributed processing to intelligent processing (figure 5.1). In the second, the development has proceeded from point-oriented computers (isolated) to line-oriented computers (family type) to area-oriented computers (network type). As these processes continue, it is hoped that computers will eventually have abilities close to human brain functions and will be used as if working with a close friend. In this sense, in both instances the objective has been to make computers more friendly to human beings.

The Development of Computer Functions

The first computer, which was developed in the United States for computing the trajectory of guns, was a single-function machine used for high-speed numerical computations. NEC's first computer was developed to execute high-speed numerical computations as well, though for circuit designs. These computers are called von Neumann machines, and they can execute

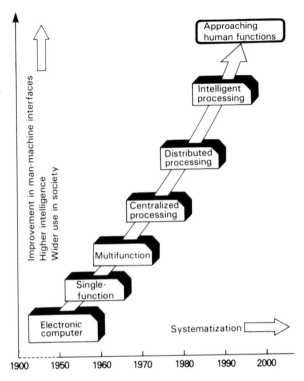

Figure 5.1
Developing trend in higher intelligence in computers

computations for many purposes merely by a change of programs. This feature provided versatility and variability which at the time the hardware did not have. When their full capabilities were recognized, computers became widely used to process large volumes of data at a very high speed.

As the computer became widely used, the multifunctional computer was developed, and such machines had wider applications. Reservation systems for airlines, trains, and hotels, on-line systems for train operation, and electrical power control systems are examples of these applications. These computer systems gather data on a real-time basis by using communications circuits, analyze the data, and provide results that are utilized in the next step of system operation.

Further development of the computer's capabilities was directed toward processing huge volumes of data for management control systems and for production control systems in plants. Such information processing called for larger-scale and higher-speed computer hardware. The higher-speed computer triggered a trend toward centralization, that is, the use of a large-scale computer to process all of the various works of many medium-size computers. This type of data processing is called centralized processing. Because of this, not only the hardware but also the programs necessary for effective operation of computer systems became increasingly larger and more complex. More recently distributed processing systems have been developed in which work is shared by a number of computers instead of all work being processed by a single computer. These systems have been particularly effective in the business world.

Now let us consider the business world. As the size of an organization increases, management and administrative support work becomes more specialized, and persons with the required skills must be hired. In addition charts need to be prepared to show the flow of information within the organizational structure.

In the case of a corporation having a head office, branch offices, sales offices, and plants or research laboratories, the normal pattern is as follows: the head office gathers data necessary for the operation of the company from the data collected by each person responsible for a particular division, the head office gives necessary directives to each division head, and then this person dispenses them with detailed instructions to the people in the division.

Today there is a great need to develop computer systems that can offer effective operations by separating and sharing functions as in actual business organizations. The information processing system based on such an idea is called the distributed processing system.

In 1974 NEC succeeded in developing its ACOS series of distributed processing computers because such systems seemed

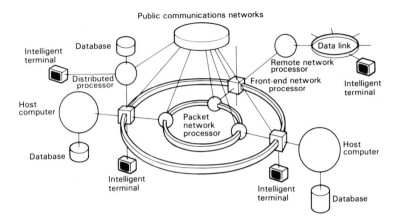

Figure 5.2
Network architecture of DINA

to represent the future direction of computers (ACOS stands for *A*dvanced *C*omputer *S*ystem). Shortly thereafter, in 1976, NEC introduced DINA. Figure 5.2 illustrates the DINA concept. DINA provides effective processing that meets the requirements of business organizations by connecting and systematizing various types of equipment, such as appropriate-size computers and terminals, through networks.

DINA has a flexible structure, so it is possible to construct any size network for it in accordance with the size and needs of the organization using it. Equipment can also be easily added or changed in the system.

Currently different countries are engaged in work on network architecture, namely the United States, Japan, and France. The International Organization for Standardization (ISO) has been developing a standard network architecture that can be interconnected to these networks. It is expected that one day all the C&C systems and equipment in the world will be interconnected.

It is said that an intelligent processing age will follow the distributed processing age. Future computers are expected to have inference functions that will mimic the process of human learning; these functions will allow the new computers to handle higher levels of decision making. With intelligent processing, computers will have taken one step closer to thinking like humans.

The notion of the intelligent computer is being taken up as one of the subjects of a national research project on fifth generation computers in Japan. At our present level of knowledge, however, we cannot even grasp at human intellectual faculties, and there are many technical problems.

The Development of Systemization Capability

Computers that were put into use in the early 1960s were usually utilized for individual tasks. Computers in this age can be called point-oriented computers. The computers that appeared next were so designed that users were able to upgrade them in accordance with the growth of their work. These computers are called family machines, or line-oriented computers. In the 1970s, with database and interactive-type processing functions in wide use, user-friendly terminals were developed. These terminals were remotely connected to computers through communication facilities. Next it became possible for users at remote locations to exchange information through time-sharing systems. These developments brought humans and computer systems closer because it became easier to use the systems; in other words, the human interface element was improved. Computers now were designed to meet the requirements of various users, and additional computers, terminals, and other equipment were available if needed. These computers are called area-oriented computers.

Office computers were developed as interactive-type systems. With this, medium or small firms that did not have access to large computer capabilities were nevertheless able to use them. These computers became powerful instruments in office automation. Sales of microcomputers rapidly increased, and with the advent of personal computers, computers have reached the general public.

As microprocessors, which are built into computer equipment and systems, progressed from 4 to 8 to 16 bits, and then to 32 bits, the capabilities of computers increased greatly. What is more, high-performance personal computers with the computation speed of 1 MIPS (million instructions per second) or more than 2 MIPS—equal to conventional mainframe computers—are beginning to appear.

Whereas conventional computers are generally considered to be large production facilities, personal computers are treated as commodities, as products for the general consumer. Even pupils in primary school are getting acquainted with the use of personal computers (sometimes they are called home computers). Now that computers have been so accepted by the public, in offices older employees and managers are learning to master them. And it is in the area of business use where the sales of personal computers are rapidly expanding. The day when only computer expert groups in EDP offices or information promotion offices wrote programs or utilized computers is long past. Now people in every business department use distributed processing computers and terminals to handle their jobs.

The different uses for computers have brought forth other areas of application. Currently receiving a lot of attention is the recent development of a super computer that has the ultra-high-speed computation abilities required for research in such fields as computational physics, computational chemistry, large-scale simulations, nonnumerical information processing, VLSI design, and meteorological information processing. What is now claimed to be the world's largest super computer can conduct floating point computations of about 1.3 billion times per second.

Thus area-oriented computers are progressing in two directions: the first is the super computer just mentioned, or database machines that effectively execute application programs using huge databases, and computer files for businesses, and the second, systems intended for personal use such as personal computers and terminals that can be remotely connected with larger computers.

Today, in the age of distributed processing, database machines and super computers are the machines used by specialists; terminals and personal computers, which are becoming able to execute a great many computations, are the machines for the general user. Those computations that cannot be handled by personal computers can be executed by large or super large computers or databases by accessing them through networks. And it will become possible to build communications network systems that transfer or exchange information by connecting office computers, word processors and various other terminals, office equipment, and telephones to meet specific work requirements.

Development of Semiconductor Devices

As advancements were made in semiconductor technology, and ICs gave way to LSIs and then LSIs to VLSIs, computer components were miniaturized, and their performance and reliability increased amazingly. The trend in the development of computer components has been to increase memory capacity while reducing size, or to increase the speed of the logic circuits that conduct basic computations for computers while reducing their size—that is, the integration of the circuits.

Figure 5.3 shows the trend in the development of memory capacity with relation to cost reduction per bit. As shown in the figure, this development was extremely rapid.

Today 256-kilobit memory chips are being produced, and 1-megabit chips are being developed. Studies on how to reduce the power consumption of integrated circuits have progressed so remarkably that power consumption has been reduced to one one-hundred-thousandth that of the first ICs. This is because the higher degree of integration results in greater heat dissipation per unit of cubic volume. Rapid progress has also been made in the development of packaging technology that controls the temperature.

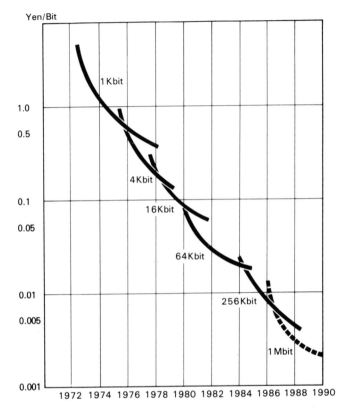

Yen/Bit

1 Kbit

1.0
0.5

4 Kbit

0.1
0.05

16 Kbit

64 Kbit

0.01

256 Kbit

0.005

1 Mbit

0.001

1972 1974 1976 1978 1980 1982 1984 1986 1988 1990

Figure 5.3
Trend in development of memory chips

The rapid reduction of power consumption in circuits has made it possible to build systems with powerful functions on one or several silicon chips. With the use of VLSI chips, called system LSIs, it has become possible to realize completely independent systems. This in turn has made it possible to realize intelligent system functions incorporating both hardware and software functions based on LSIs.

The most important progress to date in semiconductor technology has been the development of large-capacity memories and super-high-speed logic circuits of ultra small size based on digitalization and integration. These circuits have made it very easy to increase system intelligence. Moreover the number of functions computers and communications have in common, both of which have digital capabilities, has increased, and the integration of the two has become possible.

Importance of Software

Another vital element for the development of C&C is software. The volume of software has been increasing at a fast pace.

Software, or programs, used to account for most computer work. However, microprocessors (the main part of microcomputers) with built-in programs have recently been installed in various types of computers. This has greatly changed the situation. The hardware has become more flexible with built-in programs, and by changing these programs and data, the utility of these machines has been expanded. Such built-in software or programs for microprocessors is sometimes called firmware. The intelligence of robots used in automated plants can be manipulated by changing the software in their built-in microprocessors. Computers including microprocessors are now used in almost all business fields, and the volume of programs created for these machines is expanding at an annual rate of 20 to 30 percent. These machines are being increasingly diversified as well. In effect, software provides machines with the intelligence that makes the inanimate machine receptive to human use.

The target of C&C is to upgrade the man-machine interface and system intelligence by an integration of software, firmware, and hardware, using LSI/VLSI technology.

6

The Concept of Man and C&C

As we follow the history of computers and communications, we see that the purpose of research and development in these fields has been to introduce conveniences that make life richer for both the individual and society. We have to keep this always the ultimate goal of C&C—that is, to research, develop, and put into practical use products with ever wider applications that are ever more beneficial to humankind.

Now, with regard to the actual human interaction with C&C systems, it is no doubt multifaceted, as figure 6.1 shows. There are various ways humans influence C&C systems directly, as developers, sponsors, or owners, on the one hand, and users, operators, or maintenance personnel, on the other. Then there are people who do not have direct access to the systems but who will in some way be affected by them just by being a member of a society that has adopted the systems.

Introduction of the Human Factor

I have long felt that it is the human factor that should be the most essential consideration in the development of C&C systems, and this is a concept I have talked about in depth elsewhere, under the rubric Man and C&C [3].

I have chosen to visualize this concept here in a three-dimensional diagram. The development of C&C can be charted

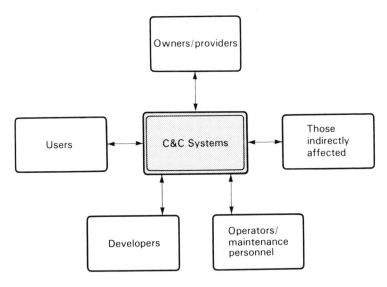

Figure 6.1
How humans will interact with C&C systems

on the X and Y axes as shown in figure 6.2. As the human factor is introduced so is a third dimension represented by the Z axis.

Humans by their complex individual makeup can have an impact on C&C technology variously. It is not possible to discuss this subject here completely, but in general, I am talking about those ingredients that characterize each person's level of thinking. It can be philosophy, ideology, emotions, behavioral mannerisms, cultural or ethnic tradition, and, not in the least, biological identity. It is, in fact, the human factor that has over the years led to the development of C&C technology and is contributing to ever new uses for the system. The human contribution to C&C is shown more explicitly in table 6.1.

First, people use C&C systems, and it is people who have influenced the softwarization of C&C and expanded its scope. Clearly then we can look forward to people wanting gradually to move on to mentally more challenging, higher-level processing

Table 6.1 Three examples of the human factor and C&C

Human factor	Index/measurement	Illustrative reference
Height of thought level	Upgrading of the man-machine interface	Figure 6.3
Degree of softwarization	Upgrading of machine intelligence	Figure 6.4
Scope of C&C system users	Wider public use of computers	Figure 6.5

activities—such as we have seen in the trend from data processing to information processing to intelligent processing. In a sense we can consider the way C&C systems are being upgraded to reflect the way thought level is upgraded in human beings. The accomplishments in man-machine interface over the years are noted in figure 6.3.

Second, hardware and software were at first developed independent of each other. With the advent of semiconductor technology the two are gradually becoming merged. In years to come there will be remarkable progress made in upgrading system intelligence through software. The development stages of softwarization are presented in figure 6.4.

When intelligent software is realized, computers and communications will be integrated in the true sense. As its forerunner, software in use today for microcomputers and personal computers is stored on cassette tapes or floppy disks and sold and circulated separately.

Third, as advancements are made in man-machine interface and software intelligence, C&C systems will become capable of being used by the general public. Already this trend can be seen. Whereas previously experts alone enjoyed the convenience of C&C, now C&C is serving a much broader cross section of people, though mainly corporations. And C&C is heading toward

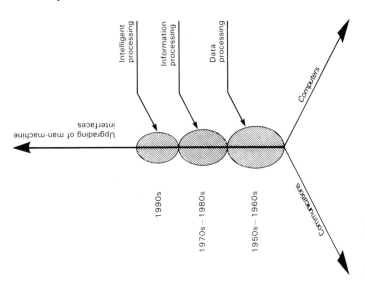

Figure 6.3
Progress in level of intelligence of C&C

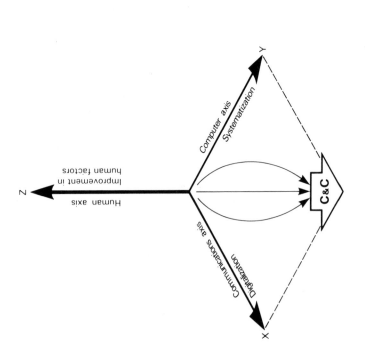

Figure 6.2
Introduction of the human axis (Z axis) to the C&C concept

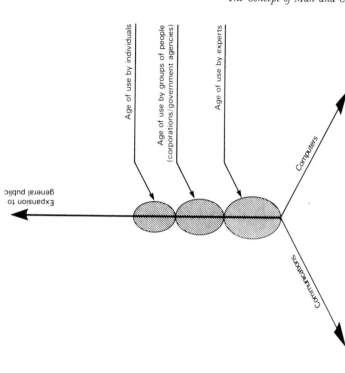

Figure 6.5
Expanding use of C&C systems

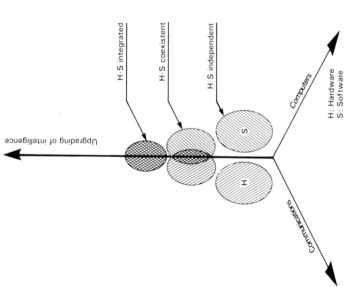

Figure 6.4
Progress in degree of softwarization of C&C

an age when it will benefit and provide remarkable living conveniences for ordinary people (figure 6.5).

When computers were introduced, they were used primarily in universities, research institutions, and large corporations. In time individual research departments or sections of these organizations were able to acquire their own minicomputers or terminals. Now many people own personal computers. Moreover microcomputers are now used in various home electronic appliances such as washing machines and air conditioners, so almost everyone is enjoying the benefits of computers even without realizing it.

The influence of the human dimension on C&C can be shown in terms of the development of the intelligent machine as in figures 6.6 and 6.7. The stages illustrated show machine systems gradually approaching humanlike functions. However, I would like to point out that human intellectual ability is advancing

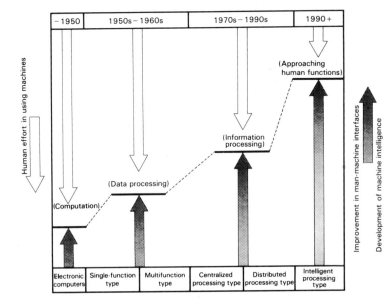

Figure 6.6
Stages leading to the intelligent machine

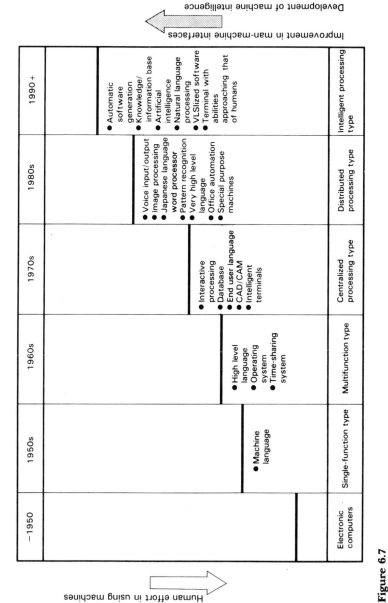

Figure 6.7
Developmental stages of C&C applications

simultaneously with advances made in the machine. I believe that the potential for human intellectual ability is so great that our present knowledge cannot define it. Therefore I think that it is extremely difficult to say that the ability of machines will ever approach that of humans.

The Effect of Stages of Machine Technology on Humans and C&C

In the late 1960s great efforts were required of humans to get maximum performance from C&C systems and machines because system intelligence and man-machine interfaces were still insufficient. This is the first stage shown in figure 6.8, where man could be said to be in C&C.

In those days lower-level computer languages were used to construct programs before the computer could be used. Such machine language, however, consisted of strings of letters, numbers, and symbols set up in patterns of communication remarkably different in structure from everyday human language, so programming was slow and troublesome. In the communications field this was the age of manual switchboards and human operators.

Today, with the advances made in system intelligence and man-machine interface, man can be said to be on C&C. Today, for example, the compiler—a program that translates programs written in human language into machine language—has been developed and is widely utilized. This has greatly facilitated programming.

Moreover the concept of database has developed to the point where it no longer just makes up data files for each program; it now has become possible to store data randomly. Further the computer is accessed no longer just by programming but by the data stored in it, allowing great progress to be made in information processing. For instance, it can handle input/output in the Japanese language, and screens are widely used for man-machine interface in daily work.

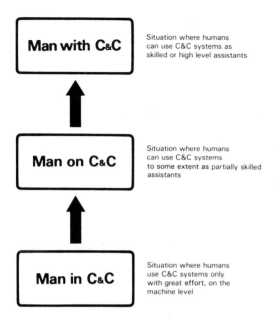

Figure 6.8
Three developmental stages of human interaction with C&C

In the communications field, as automatic telephone exchange systems advanced, it has become possible to telephone to any part of the world and also to watch TV programs from other parts of the world via satellite communications. Technological progress to date suggests a not so distant age when anyone, not just experts, will be able to use C&C systems easily; in that age man could be said to be with C&C, that is, C&C systems will play the role of skilled or high-level assistants to humans. For example, knowledge information processing functions and automatic translation functions will be developed, and systems will be able to understand the intentions and commands of humans.

In this future age it will become a matter of course to make programs using tables and diagrams, database storage (which will be equipped with stored programs, or software), and natural language, for automatic program synthesis and generation systems will be in practical use. It is expected that interaction between humans and terminals will become more natural and user-friendly.

Relationship between Humans and Systems

The task of making the interrelationship between humans and C&C systems more friendly is a particularly important one. It is a goal that research and development has continued to focus on for years. Enormous advances have already been made by utilizing C&C technologies that effectively incorporate new electronic media equipment. But, as computers become more accessible to the general public, high-performance computers may not be popular unless they are easy to use. Figure 6.9 shows how humans may use C&C systems. To help explain this, I will use the example of driving an automobile (see figure 6.10).

From the beginning the automobile was mainly designed to be a system to carry humans and their baggage. Features such as passenger driving comfort and enjoyment were relatively later developments. As shown in figure 6.10, the system "intelligence" of an automobile is the carrying function, and it consists of an engine, a body, and seats. The man-machine interface comprises the steering wheel, shift lever, pedals, and instruments. Software in a broad sense can be thought of as the various procedures involved in driving an automobile.

It is necessary for a driver to learn how to manipulate the steering wheel, the shift lever, and the pedals, how to read information indicated on the speedometer, fuel indicator, and other instruments, and how these devices mechanically interact to maintain the performance of the automobile. Moreover, because roads belong to the public, it is necessary for the driver to pay full attention to traffic regulations. This total relationship comprises the software of the automobile system.

Returning to figure 6.9, various tools have been developed to facilitate the man-machine interface for C&C systems—

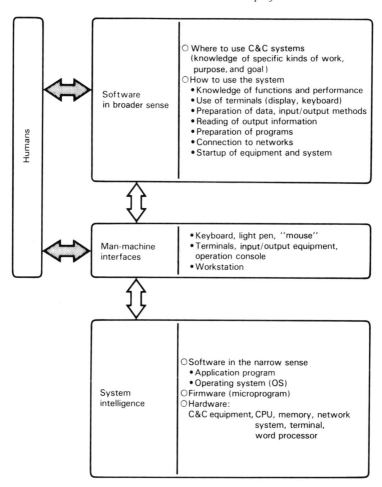

Figure 6.9
Present-day interaction between humans and C&C systems

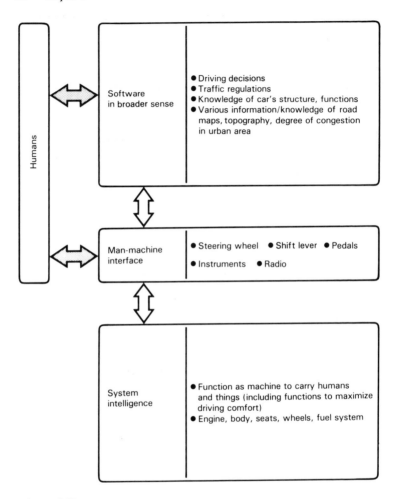

Figure 6.10
Analogy between humans interacting with C&C systems and operating an automobile

among these, display screens for personal computers and terminals, easier to understand keyboards, and light pens or a "mouse" for inputting/outputting information. Engineering workstations oriented to various specific application fields are also being developed. In addition symbols and pictures have been put into practical use in input/output operations, making the computer less intimidating for people in nontechnical fields.

Concerning software in the general sense, before C&C systems can be used, the user must have a specific kind of work for it in mind. At the same time the user must understand fully what the system can do and how to use it. This involves knowledge of functions, performance, and equipment: how to manipulate systems and terminals, how to prepare data, input/output methods, how to read output information, how to prepare programs, and how to connect to networks.

Next, let us observe how system intelligence is realized. Intelligence of systems and equipment is realized by software and hardware only in a narrow sense. Software is composed of four layers, in the order of closeness to users: individual application programs (programs providing specific functions in an individual system), basic application programs (programs for executing application functions that can be commonly used by each system), expanded basic software (new basic software functions such as language processing, pattern processing, image processing), and basic software (the program that is usually called the operating system, and functions necessary for effectively operating the system, including hardware and software). Hardware consists of the central processing unit (CPU), main memory, disks and tapes that store large volumes of data as external memory equipment, various character and graphics terminals, word processors, and facsimile equipment.

It appears now that there is need for intelligent electronic private branch exchanges (IEPBX) having advanced functions, large-capacity electronic switching systems, and equipment for network systems, including optical fiber communication systems that can transfer large volumes of information. There is also

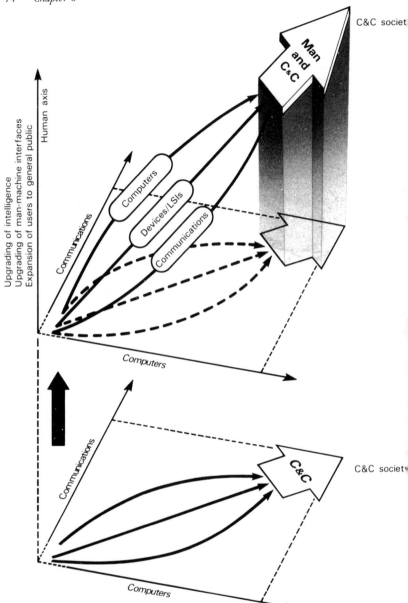

Figure 6.11
From two-dimensional to three-dimensional C&C

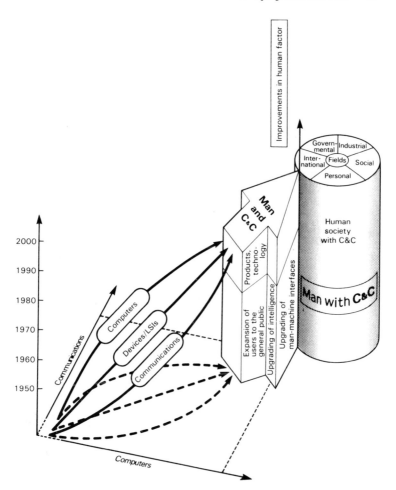

Figure 6.12
Development of man and C&C

an interest in developing so-called multifunctional intelligent terminals connecting facsimile and normal terminal operations. With the advent of LSIs, systems incorporating microcomputers have been rapidly increasing, and so has the use of firmware. Moreover there have been efforts to improve individual system intelligence by combining software, firmware, and hardware in order to maximize system functions and performance so that the objectives and needs of each use can be met.

As a forerunner of this trend, the system of incorporating read only memory (ROM)—that is, in the form of firmware, translator/executer programs for the BASIC language included in the BASIC software for personal computers—has already appeared. This is a form of "LSIization," and personal computers incorporating entire LSIized operating systems will appear in the near future.

Returning to figures 6.2 through 6.5, along the Z axis there occurs an upgrading of the man-machine interface and intelligence as well as an increase in the accessibility of computers to the general public as improvements make the computer easier to use. In figure 6.11 the lines of figure 4.1 are projected to show how the development of human interface will affect Man and C&C. The target of C&C is to create an information society with C&C infrastructure, that is, a man with C&C society that through C&C technology contributes to the enrichment of human life by providing improved systems and facilities that will affect all human activities, as shown in figure 6.12.

7

The Impact of Personal Computers and Word Processors on C&C

Personal computers have a decisive and promotive role in expanding the scope of C&C use to the general public. In particular, Japanese language word processors are intelligent machines that have the possibility of breathing new life into Japanese culture.

The Role of Personal Computers [15]

In 1984 the volume of office automation (OA) equipment marketed in Japan was 70,000 office computers, 200,000 word processors, and 1,000,000 personal computers. The number of personal computers predicted to be in operation in fiscal 1987 (April 1, 1987, to March 31, 1988) is estimated at 5 million. Assuming the total working population in Japan to be 55 million, personal computers will be used at the ratio of one per eleven persons. It is not difficult to imagine that personal computers will someday be used at the rate of one set per person, which corresponds to the present usage of TV.

On the other hand, the capabilities of large-scale computers costing some $800,000 to $1,200,000 (in U.S. dollars) twenty years ago are now available in personal computers costing just $2,800 to $4,000. The impact of the personal computer in advancing the expansion of C&C systems to the general public is expected to be enormous. Certainly it is a fact that more and more people are using personal computers. This is an interesting trend, especially for NEC which developed the personal computer in 1966. The 1966 model, called TK-80, was an 8-bit personal computer which was packaged as an assembly kit. The kit consisted of one LSI board and was aimed at educational and hobby use. If this kit was assembled in accordance with the instructions, anyone could easily build a personal computer—indeed, a truly personal computer. This personal computer kit was a sensational success, which indicated to NEC that there were many people interested in computers.

At about the same time a manufacturer in the United States began to sell personal computers and met with great success in the American market. NEC's kit product also captured the imagination of the Japanese market, and demand for personal computers expanded rapidly not only for educational and hobby purposes but also for general business use.

One of the main reasons why personal computers rapidly penetrated into the business field is that along with the progress of C&C, the demand for software development had increased so rapidly that the conventional information processing department alone was no longer able to handle the required work load. Decentralization of organizations, diversity of user requirements, and creative ideas and measures required by each organization were other major contributing factors. This is one example of how information processing has been greatly expanded to the general public by personal computers.

As opposed to the conventional process of sharing a host computer through terminals, the new role of personal computers has been to some extent to compensate for human inexperience in interfacing with C&C systems. This has helped to suggest the ultimate goal of C&C, that is, the use of computers with humans as the focal point.

Of course many people in their forties and fifties were at first afraid of the computer; "personal computer phobia," we call it. However, things have changed greatly. Today of course engineers in the forefront of research and development and even managers in the field have their own personal computers to put information in order. Also, as mentioned before, symbol and picture processing technology which is incorporated in personal computers has advanced remarkably, and graphics can easily be produced by these computers.

Personal computers are being incorporated into all sectors of society. As we see children in elementary and junior high schools actively use personal computers, we can expect a new computer culture to emerge in the next generation.

Cultural and Historical Significance of Word Processors

Located at the easternmost edge of the Asian continent, the Japanese archipelago holds many remnants and traces of cultures from Europe, the Middle East, and India as soldiers of fortune traveled through China and the Korean peninsula on the long journey from West to East. The position of Japan facing the Pacific Ocean at the easternmost edge of Asia perfectly reflects the view held one hundred years ago that "Japan is the outpost of Oriental civilization."

However, recent developments in science and technology, particularly in communications and transportation, have changed the concept of distance over the entire globe. The United States and Japan, which are separated by an endless stretch of the Pacific Ocean, now regard each other as neighbors. The two countries also have become culturally very close.

Today Japan is no longer considered the terminus of Oriental civilization; rather the country has become a western cultural starting point for the Orient, a point where East meets West. In looking back on the development of Japanese civilization, I believe that it is very important to consider the role of the word processor in the Japanese language.

I am not a position to explain in detail the origin of the Japanese language, but it is said that the Japanese language did not utilize written characters or letters in the beginning, but rather that the culture was handed down verbally from generation to generation. The Chinese culture, including Chinese literature, was conveyed to Japan in the eighth century in what is known as the Nara period, and it had a tremendous influence on the Japanese. Although the Chinese and Japanese languages were essentially different in structure, Chinese characters were adopted for writing, and for the first time Japan had a mode of written expression. With this, Japan's precious cultural assets such as *Kojiki* ("Myths and Ancient History"), *Nihon Shoki* ("The Chronicals of Japan"), and *Manyoshu* ("Collections of Poems") were prepared.

The thousands of poems in the *Manyoshu*, however, were written in the *Manyo kana* which was particularly epoch-making for Chinese characters were used to express Japanese sounds. This led to the creation of phonetic *kana* characters. It is no exaggeration to say that the invention of phonetic *kana* script by Master Kobo, wherein pronunciations of the Japanese language were expressed in symbols, was the greatest achievement in ancient Japan. This was the motive force for the Japanese culture to develop up to its present level.

Thanks to *kana*, which consists of forty-eight phonetic letters, the Japanese language, with its unique feature of composing sentences by the mixture of Chinese characters and *kana* script, could be established, and the Japanese culture spread to the general public. The Japanese language too could now easily accept foreign languages as long as they were expressed in *kana*. The recent development of the word processor can be said to have profound cultural and historical significance similar to the invention of Japanese *kana* about 1,000 years ago, which in fact triggered the spread of the Japanese language from the nobles to the people of the entire nation.

English is the most widely used language in the world. That the language consists of only twenty-six alphabetical letters, has relatively simple grammatical structure, and is easy to pronounce may be why it is so widely used. The invention and spread of English language typewriters facilitated not only the proliferation of written documents but also contributed to making the computer more accessible to the U.S. public. In effect, both the typewriter and the computer keyboard have been instrumental in advancing the information age.

The reason why I say that the Japanese language word processor is an intelligent machine that will greatly influence Japan's culture is that it provides functions fundamentally different from Japanese language typewriters. The conventional Japanese language typewriter is very slow in keying speed and is so complex that it cannot be compared with an English language typewriter.

The Japanese language word processor can input *kana* (both *hiragana* and *katakana*), the English alphabet, numerals, symbols, and Chinese characters, has systems to convert regular *kana* or romanized *kana* to Chinese characters, and can store idioms in the memory unit. Moreover a major feature of this word processor is that it has various editing functions that can be controlled by human instructions. These functions enable us to execute a wide variety of tasks, such as combining, deleting, or editing sentences, integrating different documents, or using various documents as reference sources.

This machine has several outstanding features. It takes full advantage of the flexibility of the Japanese language by writing horizontally or vertically, it can freely insert mathematical equations or numerals, it can express foreign words in *katakana* as well as sentences consisting of Chinese characters and *kana*, and, finally, it can include English or other foreign words in Japanese sentences when necessary.

Here I would like to touch on a proposal for new keyboard arrangements which match the features of Japanese language structure. NEC's M-type keyboard input system, newly developed by Masasuke Morita, takes into regard the fact that most of the Chinese characters in Japanese sentences are idioms having phonetic readings and that when these phonetic readings are expressed in romanization, they can be classified based on their regularity. Key arrangements match the shape of human hands according to ergonomic considerations. With this system users can more easily remember the input operations, and input

Keyboard for M-type Japanese language word processor developed by M. Morita of NEC in 1979

speed is approximately doubled while operator fatigue is reduced.

By partially upgrading the functions of the Japanese language word processor, it will be possible to obtain the function of a personal library. Users can use this library by recording various information resources in an LSI ROM (read only memory), or an optical disk, and by changing the information memory media as necessity arises. Moreover it will become possible to make hard copies of required portions easily.

When we consider the word processor in this way, it can be said to be a highly intelligent auxiliary information machine for humans. The functions of word processors have expanded to fields centering on nonnumerical information and knowledge. This is in contrast to the fact that computers initially were used primarily for numerical computations. The Japanese language word processor is an intelligent machine possessing infinite possibilities.

8

Software: The Problem and the Solution

State of the Art

For more people to be able to use C&C systems in different ways, it is essential that software be used effectively. Demand for software is increasing annually, and so is the number of people engaged in producing software. Still, many problems are arising in major advanced countries because software production cannot catch up with demand due to the shortage of software engineers. It is quite certain that with our present technological standards and production systems, this software crisis will continue for a long time. Even if the possibility of enriching human life with C&C technology exists, it will not be realized unless the demand for software, which serves as its basis, can be met.

To eliminate these problems, we must try to understand and examine in detail the present situation concerning software production, maintenance, and services. It is vitally important that we begin this effort today.

Measures for Improving the Quality and Productivity of Software

The rapid spread of microcomputers into almost all industrial fields, in addition to information processing, is a major cause

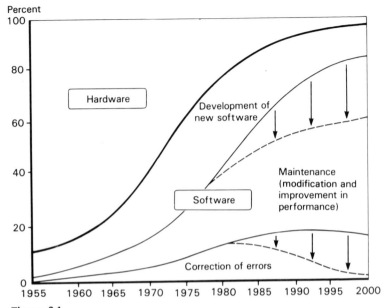

Figure 8.1
Solving software problems

of the conspicuous increase in the cost of software. Changes in the cost ratio of software versus hardware in systems using computers are shown in figure 8.1. From the figure you can see that the percentage of software costs is rapidly increasing. Moreover, because more than 70 percent of software engineers are engaged in maintaining the huge amount of software already developed, there is a tendency to delay new development work. The concept of software maintenance here is generally different from hardware maintenance, for it pertains to the removal of defects found in the software during its use, modification of software to meet new requirements, and work to improve performance.

If the technology of software development and maintenance remains at the present level, within a few years, it will become almost impossible to satisfy the demand for software development. It is expected that the software crisis which has been felt in numerous areas in recent years will expand to all industries. Realizing fundamental reforms in the technologies for software production, management, and quality control will soon become a major task.

Appropriate measures in the standardization and modularization of software, as well as in the production and distribution of packaged software, will greatly improve the productivity and quality of software. It is also necessary to tackle the matter of maintenance with a more forward-looking attitude than presently prevails, and it will further become more important to improve the productivity and quality of maintenance work.

Software production can now be basically characterized as a hands-on industry. Software is said to be a product of mental labor, but each production process clearly requires careful hand operations. This has been a major cause of bugs being introduced that affect the quality of software. Moreover it is known that the level of software production and quality varies greatly from one developer to another. It is said that individual abilities of programmers differ by a factor of 1 to 25 or 30 and that the abilities of development teams often by 1 to 4.

For these reasons it is necessary to enlighten and educate software engineers so that they work to develop methods for efficient design, manufacture, and testing of software. Also software engineers must strive to standardize work, to prepare tools useful for development and maintenance, and to modernize the work environment. It will be necessary to apply the knowledge of human engineering to these areas.

The physical environment has an important role to play in improving software development. It is important to determine measures for improving the workplace conditions for software work. This indicates that attention should be paid to such details as the sizes and shapes of desks, the dimensions and spaciousness of production and computer testing rooms, the arrangements of files and terminals, conference rooms, and programming rooms. In addition studies comparing the quality of software work by individuals with that of teams are important as well as studies of how effective development teams can be assembled.

Modernization of Software Plants by C&C

The NEC Corporation has already begun modernizing software production systems by introducing large numbers of terminals into software plants in order to improve design, manufacture, and inspection methods using interactive-type software production systems. Because this introduces "equipment" of C&C technology, we call it the "equipping of software."

Factory automation is steadily progressing in major hardware industries, where computer capabilities have become successfully utilized in every department—namely design, production, inspection, shipping, and distribution. Because of their power, computers are making spectacular contributions to CAD, CAM, automatic production systems, robotics, production control, and distribution control.

This modernization of hardware has been promoted during the past twenty years, making possible the improvements in productivity we see today. However, progress in the software production process is invisible. It will be important for software engineers to establish new software production systems and maintenance service systems by candidly accepting the good points of hardware production, maintenance, and services, by changing their conceptions without adhering to past thinking, and by developing original methods in the areas that are different from hardware systems.

I personally believe that as in the case of hardware production, software production is not difficult and that more than 90 percent of software can be produced by rationalizing work processes and utilizing modern facilities supported by computers.

I compare the development of software with climbing Mt. Fuji, the highest mountain in Japan (figure 8.2). By volume, 90 percent of the mountain lies below the fifth station, which anyone can easily reach by car or bus. However, the remaining 10 percent, from the fifth station up, must be climbed on foot. This is true mountaineering, where physical strength and vigor are required.

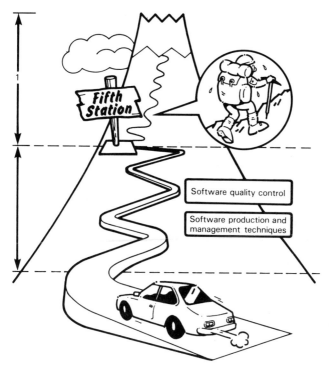

Figure 8.2
Analogy between software production and climbing Mt. Fuji

I believe that it is possible to produce effectively the majority of software by adopting new methods (by the automobile analogy in chapter 6, paved roads) and by using good tools (by the same analogy, automobiles). As in other fields it will be possible to standardize and modularize software in producing that 90 percent of the volume that corresponds to the part of the mountain below the fifth station, and it will also be possible to apply production and management techniques. There is much room for modernization and improvement in this area, and this is also the area where large gains can be achieved by equipping the workplace with terminals and computers.

In contrast, the software above the fifth station is small in quantity, yet it includes advanced and innovative software, namely knowledge information processing systems and software for automatic language translation. These are fields that have yet to be explored, and we will need to exert our full intellectual powers to develop these new types of software.

Next, let us consider the importance of improving quality. As I described at the beginning of the book, I devoted myself to improving quality in the communications equipment manufacturing industry just after the war. Subsequently, for the purpose of manufacturing defect-free products, I initiated the Zero Defects (ZD) movement in the company, and we were successfully able to meet the challenges of improving quality and reliability of hardware for communications equipment, computers, and semiconductors.

Several years ago, after I called on all employees to initiate improvement activities in software, companywide Software Quality Control Group Activities (SWQC or SWQC-GA) were established. These activities now enjoy the enthusiastic participation of 10,000 software personnel in 1,700 groups. Here too achievements have been remarkable.

To foster further a modern software industry, it will be necessary to strengthen computer support as much as possible in software work, particularly in the analysis of requirements for design work which thus far has been almost completely done by hand. In the most advanced areas of software development, improvements in productivity and quality are being made by providing more than one terminal per person.

There was a time when software could be prepared with paper and pencil. Now, however, software production has developed into a kind of equipment-intensive industry, with completely different characteristics from how software was originally conceived.

As shown in figure 8.3, in the 1960s software was produced using high-level languages. In the 1970s various new methods were tried, and in 1980s these methods have led to the advent

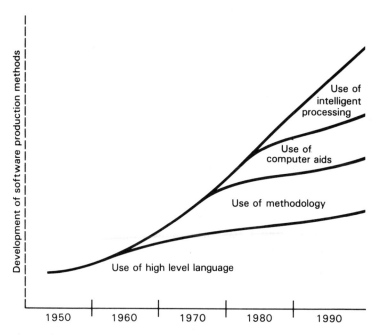

Figure 8.3
Development of software production methods

and use of personal computers, terminals, workstations, and other powerful tools. In the late 1980s, as knowledge information processing functions are introduced, integrated software workstations with high intelligence will be realized, and then, by utilizing the workstations effectively, new software production/ maintenance support systems will be established.

We have to pay special attention to the fact that software consists of more than programs. The quality of documents and support services is also important and must be improved if software is to satisfy users. The quality of documents is very important for the maintenance of software. Manuals are the image software presents to customers—and it is essential that they be easy to understand.

Software Development Environment and Intelligent Facilities

The way software is often prepared today in labor-intensive work environments, the level of software development can be said to be at a period of infancy in the industrial life cycle. However, some companies have made efforts to improve software production and management techniques, and in these places the labor-intensive work environment is rapidly giving way to a more intellectually oriented environment. Attempts at improving production methods have included promoting reassessment and automation of software development and finding better means for production and quality control of software. Further there has been some experimentation with distributed-type work environments to take the place of the current centralized type.

The work-at-home, or telecommuting, system has been proposed as one example of a distributed-type workplace. In Japan, however, because of the labor situation and housing environment, many problems prevent the achievement of a genuine home-working system. In place of this a satellite office system has been proposed.

The satellite office is an office established for a specific purpose near workers' houses. The office is connected to the software plant and the head office by full-capacity communications circuits. In this office environment one is able to work as if working at a plant. I think that the satellite office has a great possibility of becoming the new office pattern in the C&C age, particularly, in Japan (figure 8.4).

Present software plants are equipped with various types of software development equipment that are connected to central computers. Software was once regarded as works of art produced by specialists having a high level of technical ability. By crystalizing the procedures of these specialists, and compiling them into a database, it may someday be possible to create expert systems combining the technical know-how of many skilled software engineers.

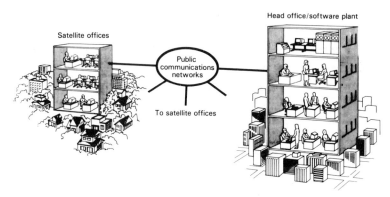

Figure 8.4
Satellite offices

When software was developed using general-purpose computers, the facilities used were the same as those on which developed programs were run. Therefore it was possible to test the programs (both the programs and the system) using one set of facilities. However, the growth in demand for software is much higher for built-in-type software for microprocessors incorporated in industrial and consumer electronics products than it is for general-purpose computers.

Therefore the present software development facilities are often different from those for testing or actual usage. This suggests that modern software plants must include equipment and functions for conducting simulation tests.

Another characteristic of software production is that accuracy and clarity of expression are required. If vagueness or unsettled details are allowed to remain in the specifications for software functions, misunderstandings or errors in conveying the user's intentions are caused, and software errors, or "bugs," may be included in the programs. Therefore some way has to be found for software developers to better perceive customers needs. One way may be to use machines that transmit face-to-face conversations, which, interestingly enough, aid mutual communication because they reveal nonverbalized feelings through various facial or bodily expressions or nuances. Means of information transfer that convey graphics or pictures, such as telemeeting or teleconferencing systems, are effective for the transfer of such human information. Of course there are various formats for the transfer of information or intentions, such as images, text, and codes. C&C equipment will be provided with a means of transfer for each of these formats.

International Cooperation for Software Development

Many countries are still at the developing stage of C&C. However, if these countries try to modernize industries to improve productivity by introducing computer and communications technologies, they will first have to train a considerable number of software engineers. It would be a significant step forward to consider international technological cooperation between countries already facing the limits of their development ability and countries that have yet to acquire this ability. In contrast to hardware, great material resources are not needed for software development. The major resource required is competent engineers. This is the feature of software that deserves the greatest attention.

Examples of technical cooperation among countries that can have a substantial effect include pioneering C&C application systems such as the use of the space resources, seabed resources exploration systems, and food development management systems. In order to keep these systems functioning, it may become necessary to gather information by communications satellites or to establish analysis centers that specialize in advanced technology. Effective development of such pioneering systems will be possible if each country cooperates in the technical field in which it is strongest.

The development of C&C technology—particularly with regard to the position of man and C&C technology which can be realized through the spread of modern communications worldwide—will greatly change the face of international cooperation.

For example, it will be possible to conduct the allotted work in each country without all the people involved in the projects being physically present.

It is clear that such international cooperation will become more important as economic cooperation between nations improves. However, to expand C&C systems, preliminary preparations are needed, such as any of the following: advanced countries could provide technical training for students from other countries, they could provide technical assistance in software by sending teams of engineers to these countries, or they could establish companies specializing in software development through the cooperation of native companies.

Still, producing software has traditionally been a very individual affair, and a true distribution of labor has not yet been fully realized. Therefore, before international cooperation in software development can take place, facilities will need to be developed that can communicate between remote regions and establish an entirely new work system that breaks down software development into tasks. Further there will also need to be developed an educational system that will make it easy for the people to learn about the software in C&C technology.

NEC has already established cooperation with several countries in such ways. NEC has learned that to develop a healthy cooperative relationship, it is desirable to advance appropriate systems in a form compatible with the stage of development of each country. These activities should also be based on mutual trust and cooperation and undertaken in a spirit of promoting mutual benefits.

In the case of application software, it is important to keep the following point in mind: each country is unique in its organizations, systems, and culture; truly usable systems can be expected only when users are interested in and involved from the stage of deciding specifications that meet their requirements and cooperate until they are fully satisfied. From this viewpoint it is obvious that the most effective method is to develop basic application software that relates to the areas in which each country wishes to use computers. This is an important aspect of software technology cooperation with such countries, and this approach will be helpful in effectively fostering the ability to develop technology in them.

9

Modern Communications

My view of the future development of C&C, which I focus on communications and thus call "modern communications," is an elaboration of the talk I was invited to give at the Fourth World Telecommunications Forum held in October 1983 under the auspices of the International Telecommunication Union [5].

I use the term "modern communications" to refer mostly to the twenty-first century. But I include in my discussion present-day intelligent information communications that abundantly incorporate computer technology. Naturally telecommunications network systems used as infrastructures for the circulation of information will play a central role, as will the broadening of and improvement in levels of information handling in conventional telecommunications services, including broadcasting services. Also there will be more efficient methods of handling conventional nontelecommunication services, such as the replacement of mail and publication/distribution with electronic mail and electronic files. Related to these developments are the applications of computer technology to communications facilities and new communications media.

The outlook for modern communications encompasses various technological trends related to information communication networks and their application service systems. The following are representative examples: the integrated service digital network (ISDN), the value-added network (VAN), the direct broadcast satellite system (DBS), videotex (CAPTAIN in Japan), office automation (OA), the corporate communication systems local area network (LAN), and the wide area network (WAN).

The scope of modern communications will be much wider than that of conventional communications. But basically it will concern an expansion in scope of the three fundamental functions of information handling. Contributing to this development will be various forms of human interface for all information media.

Fundamental Functions of Information Handling

To make the development of modern communications easier to understand from the standpoint of the C&C concept, I have singled out the following three functions as the essential elements of modern communications:

• information generation,
• information transfer,
• information storage.

The first element, information generation, involves the task of preparing information to be transmitted in a form easily understood by the receiver. This includes processing or converting information by using computers. The second element, information transfer, occurs as information is delivered to remote destinations quickly (at the speed of electromagnetic waves) without error, which is of course the basic function of conventional telecommunications. The third element, information storage, files and collates information for later use (not immediately after processing/conversion and transmission/receiving) by the computer. The interrelationship of these three functions is expressed in figure 9.1. This classification scheme is based on one used for the functional analysis, arrangement, and synthesis of office automation (OA) systems. Applied to modern communications, it covers the entire breadth of the information society. Its functional elements can be further broken down as follows:

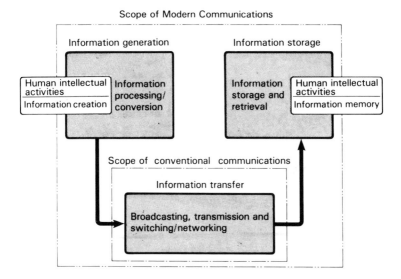

Figure 9.1
The functions of modern communications

- *Information generation*   Creation, processing, conversion, editing, analysis, computation, synthesis, etc.
- *Information transfer*   Broadcasting, transmission, switching, networking, reception, signal processing, collection, display, etc.
- *Information storage*   Storage, retrieval, memory, etc.

As figure 9.1 shows, human beings are the source and final destination of information. In conventional communication the pattern of flow proceeds from information generation to information transfer to information storage. However, there may be other sources and destinations of information in modern communications. One such example is the case of information being detected, sensed, and taken from the natural environment by various information machines or physical material flow and energy flow handling machines serving as information sources. The second is the case where the recipient of the information

directly controls machines that handle physical material flow
or energy flow based on the information received.

Information Generation

Information is generated, first, from thoughts that arise and
take shape in the human mind as words, sentences, or pictures.
Included in this function are the writing and editing of reports
to be transmitted in verbal (face-to-face or by telephone) or
letter form (by mail, telex, or facsimile) as part of day-to-day
business and social transactions. Also included are creative ideas
leading to discoveries and inventions in science and technology,
and the production of works of art.

An essential activity of human beings then is to create, plan,
and compose. One of the features of the modern life, however,
is that intelligent equipment that assists human beings in doing
such jobs is coming into wide use. As more applications are
found for various information processing equipment such as
personal computers and intelligent terminals, there is greater
demand for computer technologies such as word processing,
graphics processing, and computer-aided design (CAD). In other
words, information processing and conversion are an intrinsic
part of information generation.

Information Transfer

Information transfer involves a process peculiar to conventional
telecommunications. It is represented here in figure 9.2, which
is taken from a famous paper on communication theory entitled
"The Mathematical Theory of Communication," published in
1948 by C. E. Shannon of Bell Telephone Laboratories. In the
figure the flow of messages from the transmission side to the
reception side corresponds to the information transfer section
of figure 9.1.

Today, with the development of satellite communications
and long-distance optical submarine cable system technologies,
truly great strides have been made in global information transfer
technology. Therefore the main feature of information transfer
in modern communications may be said to be global coverage.

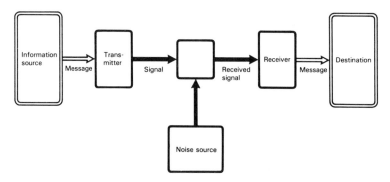

Figure 9.2
Schematic of a conventional communication system (C.E. Shannon 1948)

One of the major requirements of information transfer is that it be done without error. This means that transmitted information must be received in the same form in which it is generated and at the right destination. This requires reliable transmission channels and switching equipment. Communications networks that combine the two are said to be transparent.

We use the term "transparent communications" here to refer to traditional communications such as the telephone and TV broadcasting which transmit the voice or images unaltered to the listener or viewer. Transparent communications are but one part of modern communications. The scope of modern communications will be enlarged to include, besides transparent communications, intelligent or "value-added" communications which incorporate information generation and storage and thus surpass the capabilities of transparent communications. I will touch on this in the next chapter.

Information Storage
Previously information storage was described as a procedure that files and collates information for later utilization (not immediately after processing/conversion) by the computer. The fact is, however, information storage (or memory) and infor-

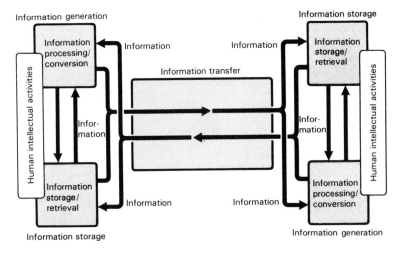

Figure 9.3
Cycles of information flow

mation generation are actually two sides of the same coin, which can be explained by considering the following two points:

1. As information is generated, many electronic cycles of information generation and storage are running. The process may be compared with that of refining the final draft of a paper, for which the author might refer to pieces of information in his or her memory, notebook, or word processor.

2. Before the generated information can be effectively used, it must be stored in the recipient's memory equipment in retrievable form.

The various cycles involved in the generation and storage of information are shown in figure 9.3. With relation to the flow of information shown in figure 9.2, this cycle may be understood as generation–transfer–storage–generation.

There are also storage functions included in the transfer function. Examples include shared information storage functions installed in the information transfer routes for electronic messaging/mail systems and in electronic file and library systems.

In a sense information storage incorporates a kind of information transfer function too. But unlike the transfer function which transfers information geographically over an interval of space, it transfers information after an interval of time. More precisely, the information transfer function can be said to involve a kind of spacewise transfer and the information storage function, a kind of timewise transfer.

Information Media as Viewed from the Human Interface

The primary way of conveying thoughts is to speak a language using the mouth to produce a voice which is heard through the ear. Thoughts can be expressed by hand in the form of pictures, codes, letters, or sentences for another party to read using the eyes. There are, in addition, ways of showing thoughts by facial expressions or bodily gestures, which are also seen by the eyes.

The various types of media that handle information generated by the human voice, hand, or body have been classified as shown at the left-hand side of figure 9.4. But with further development of the computer, the classification scheme may become more fluid, especially with regard to the position of computer graphics and animation in the future.

Arranged horizontally in this figure are the three information-handling functions shown in figure 9.1. Observe how the areas of conventional communications in figure 9.1 relate to those of modern communications, which include conventional communications, shown in figure 9.4. Conventional communications primarily involve information transfer, and the media include the voice, numerical data, sentences, and various still and moving images, such as are in this figure. Yet, from the standpoint of modern communications, all three information-handling functions—information transfer, information generation, and information storage—must be considered equally.

As the arrows on each side of the conventional communications box show, conventional communications is not static, it is developing as C&C. One example is the recent research and

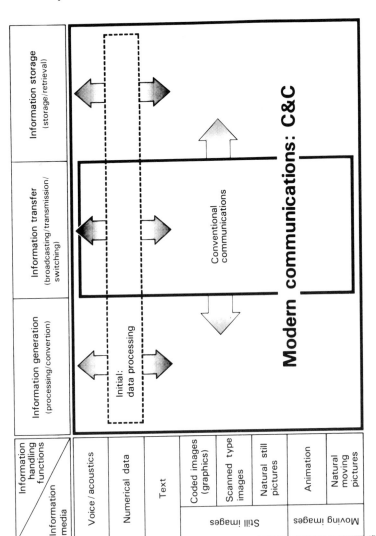

Figure 9.4
Modern communications incorporating functional areas of C&C

development to produce a new network composition utilizing recent digital communication technology. There are also standardization activities being pursued by CCITT, which is an organ of the International Telecommunication Union (ITU). It has been proposed by CCITT that the 64-kilobit per second integrated digital network (IDN) based on telephone networks be expanded to the integrated service digital network (ISDN).

The numerical data category at the left-hand side of the figure, in fact, extends into the oblong area enclosed by dashed lines. This was initially the activity of computers, or rather, electronic data processing (EDP) systems. At its developing stage the computer was capable of executing all three functions of information handling, although its coverage of information transfer facilities was limited. The applications of data processing systems have been expanding upward and downward, as indicated by the arrows in the figure, to all the information media categories. When this process is completed, we will be in the modern communications era.

Various Facets of Modern Communications Systems

The evolution of modern communications will surpass in scope conventional telecommunications in a great variety of ways. Developments that suggest this era can already be seen in at least the ten areas of telecommunications I enumerate here.

Domestic Communications and International Communications   Economic restrictions posed by time and geographical distance are being reduced through satellite communications systems. Still, work needs to be done to overcome differences in language and time zones. This is a task for international communication organizations to accomplish along with improvements in the transfer of wideband information of pictures, for example, and the standardization of interfaces.

Voice, Data, and Graphics Communications   The current construction of integrated services digital networks will provide the facilities for integrating to a greater extent the transmission and switching operations of various information media.

Fixed-Point and Mobile Communications Both fixed-point and mobile communication systems are becoming available for transmitting information over long distances. Utilizing the radio, which is an indispensable mobile communication medium, small-zone systems and multichannel access (MCA) systems are now being used with automobile telephone systems.

Broadcasting and Point-to-Point Communications Service Communications services can be classified according to the direction in which their information transfer occurs. They are called uni-directional in the case of broadcasts, which are made from one-to-many points, or bidirectional, where point-to-point communications are involved. In the case of television broadcasting systems, to meet growing needs to expand and improve service areas, information volume, and broadcasting quality, direct broadcasting satellites (DBS) and cable television (CATV) are being introduced.

Public and Business Communications Public communications networks must be installed and operated to maintain uniform nationwide service. In contrast, private communications companies may install communications networks that connect specific information sources to specific destinations for reasons of company profit.

Person-to-Person Communications, Person-to-Information Machine Communications, and Communications between Information Machines. Different kinds of human interactions are possible at both the source and destination points of a communication. Office and factory automation equipment is continually being installed, leading to ever wider use of computers. Therefore the weight of person to information machine communication and information machine to information machine communication is increasing compared to conventional person-to-person communication by telephone.

On-Demand Immediate Communications and Store and Forward Communication Services The length of time it takes for information from the sender to reach the recipient depends on whether the generated information is immediately transferred to the other party or is transferred at an appropriate time after being stored and memorized once by the sender or recipient or by machine along the transfer route. Store and Forward (S&F) communication services will become necessary to overcome situations where the recipient is not immediately available to receive the information or where there is congestion along the transfer route. Such S&F communication service is an example of information processing/storage, or value-added, communications to be described shortly.

Recorded and Nonrecorded Communications   Occasionally it is necessary to reuse generated information or information transferred to the recipient, after a time interval. The telephone is an example of nonrecorded communication. Editing generated information by word processor, and then storing it, or producing hard copies of messages received through communications between workstations, telex communications, and facsimile communication are examples of recorded communications.

On-Demand (Random Occurrence) and Scheduling (Reservations) Communications   A request for information transfer to communications networks is often based on the time the request is made. Whether on-demand (random occurrence) or scheduling (reservations) communication is used depends on the activities of the persons who are the senders or recipients of information, the functions of the information machines, the characteristics of the information itself—for example, a unidirectional multiple communication of the same message or a one-to-one bidirectional communication—and the status of use of the transfer route.

Transparent and Value-Added (Information Processing/Storage) Communications   Transparent communications ensure the transfer of various forms of information such as voices or numerical data in their pure form from an information source to a destination. In value-added communications, information is not simply transferred, it is communication-processed by computer functions interspersed in the communications network. Data format conversion and storage are examples of this. Furthermore information processing service functions, including computation processing and database storage and retrieval in and out of the network, can be embedded. This is called VAN (Value-Added Network) communications.

Composition of Modern Communications Systems

It is not possible to show in a diagram all the areas contributing to a global modern communications system which I cover in the preceding section. In figure 9.5 I have attempted to meet that challenge. The overall scheme, however, can be depicted in various ways, depending on where the emphasis is placed. I have chosen to express it in its broadest sense as a combination of three functional blocks:

• terminals interfacing with humans,

• conventional transparent communications networks,

• information service centers based on computer functions.

In the center of the figure I have placed conventional domestic transparent communications networks. These are connected to the domestic transparent communications networks of other countries via various international transparent communications networks (such as international satellite and international terrestrial communications systems). These are shown at the right-hand side of the figure.

Both domestic and international transparent communications networks have multilayered structures that include public telephone networks, public packet communication networks, and various leased lines. Such multilayered structuring is considered to be important not only for service functions but also for work assignments and cooperative arrangements among enterprises. I will explain this in more detail later.

Shown at the left-hand side of figure 9.5 are typical home systems, whose number could equal the number of homes, and on-premise business systems, which are fewer in number but

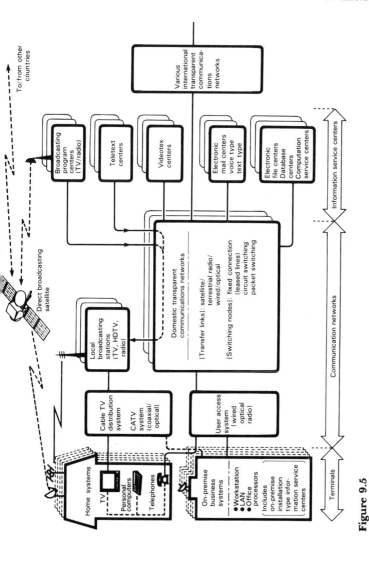

Figure 9.5
Overall composition of modern communications systems possible with C&C technologies

could equal the number of offices and plants. Of course all the possibilities cannot be included in the figure, but a TV receiver, a telephone, and a personal computer are shown as the most common home system terminals. Representative of on-premise business systems are a workstation (WS), a local area network (LAN), which is a general term for an on-premise communication network, and an office processor, which is a general term for shared information (processing and storage) equipment. The workstation considered here includes conventional telephones, personal computers, word processors, and other business terminals.

As shown in the figure, these home systems and on-premise business systems are connected to domestic and international communications networks via user access systems centered on telephone subscriber lines. Standardizing the interface between the user access systems and home or business systems is an important objective of studies on integrated services digital networks (ISDN) being conducted by the International Telecommunication Union (ITU) for the parallel development of digital public telephone and other networks.

In the home system, cable- and radio-type broadcasting program distribution systems are important communications media in parallel with public telephone subscriber (user) access systems. An example of a cable-type system is the CATV distribution system, which is also shown in the illustration as cable TV distribution systems. The radio-type system includes direct broadcasting satellite systems. These distribution systems deal mainly with the reception of the video and audio programs broadcast by program centers through local stations. In addition unbalanced bidirectional transmission systems are currently being developed. In these systems the downward flow of information to home systems is much larger than the upward flow of information to the centers, which is what is meant by the term "unbalanced."

Arranged in a vertical row between the domestic and international transparent communication networks in figure 9.5 are function boxes noting the various information service centers, such as broadcasting program centers and teletext centers, connected to domestic communications networks. These can be collectively called information service centers. This is because they are remote and shared-type facilities for general use by the many users of modern communications systems. Various high-level information processing and storage functions are available at these facilities.

The concept of the so-called value-added networks (VAN) includes networks for reselling transfer functions. However, these networks must include remote and shared-type information processing and information storage facilities as value-adding facilities to be used for business purposes. As in figure 9.1, the information generation and storage functions shown in this figure correspond mainly to the various information service centers and intelligent functional portions of terminals, and the information transfer function corresponds mainly to various levels of transparent communications networks.

Moreover the home and business systems shown in figure 9.5 are installed as terminal systems. In this respect mobile communications systems, such as automobile telephones or paging systems used mainly outdoors, would be separate terminal systems. However, cordless telephones, cordless data terminals, and various remote control devices are available today, so mobile communications exist not only outdoors but also in home and business systems.

Figure 9.6 illustrates in more detail the different transmission systems shown in figure 9.5. In the figure the terminals for home systems are shown on the right, and those for business systems on the left. Various information service centers are shown on both the right and left along with a breakdown of their specific functions. Communications processing and information processing centers for VANs are also indicated. Mobile communication terminals, which are left out of figure 9.5, are shown in the upper left-hand corner of this figure.

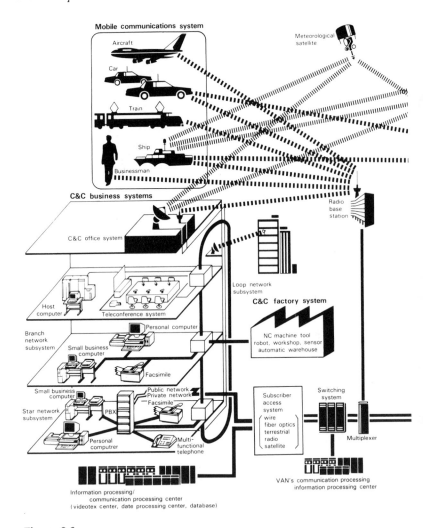

Figure 9.6
Detailed composition of modern communications systems possible with
C&C technologies

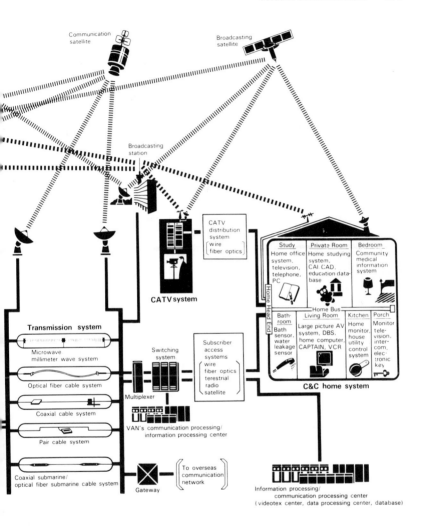

Matrix Structures of C&C Systems

As I have mentioned previously, the concept of modern communications is related directly to the future development of telecommunications systems based on the concept of C&C. However, the general concept of C&C can be used to understand much broader social structures, which include communications systems. C&C-type social systems can be considered applicable in public, business, and home systems.

Each of these three fields will contribute to the structure of a multilayered information society. Of course modern communications systems are incorporated in various forms in the constituent elements of the structure. This is shown somewhat abstractly in figure 9.7 as a single-matrix structure. I proposed this concept of the matrix and multilayered structure for the first time in 1982 at the special lecture delivered before the general meeting of the alumni association of the Massachusetts Institute of Technology. The three functional blocks shown at the top of this figure are connected with the entire C&C system. This structure is derived from figure 9.5. Of course terminals (equipment interfacing with humans), communications networks (on-premise, wide area, etc.), and computers (information service centers having functions of information generation and storage) are the major components of modern communications, as mentioned in the previous section.

Multilayered Structure of Communications Networks

Let us turn our attention again to the composition of communications networks as one element of the matrix structure of C&C system.

In each country the structure of telecommunication networks is different because of differing needs and influences. However, when this process is viewed together with the development of C&C technology and service applications, any communications network can be seen to comprise a multilayered structure. Taking

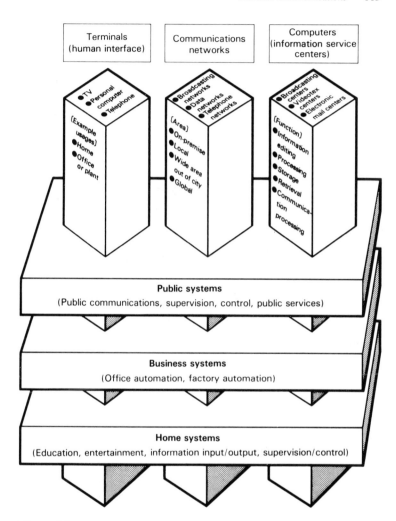

Figure 9.7
Matrix structure of C&C systems

this one step further, modern communications systems, which are themselves based on the C&C concept, can also be understood to tend toward a multilayered structure.

The multilayered structure of communications networks reflects the variety of information to be handled. It also reflects the state of the multilayered composition of various C&C systems. The relationship between this multilayered structure and the variety of information handled can be viewed from different angles.

In discussing the multilayered structure of communications networks, I would like to focus on domestic transparent communications networks, excluding terminals and information service centers. These are illustrated in figures 9.5, 9.6, and 9.7, which I have already explained, and in figure 9.8 which I will now introduce.

There are various ways of determining the composition of a layer in a multilayered structure. However, I have suggested the three layers shown in figure 9.8 after considering the present state of communications networks in advanced countries.

The Public Communications Networks Layer

Public national infrastructure networks connect information sources and destinations located throughout a nation. This network is established to provide uniform nationwide service, whatever the economies of the enterprise in some regions. Improvement of operation functions is the primary requirement of these networks. Examples include conventional public telephone switching networks and public digital data switching networks (such as packet communications networks and circuit switching networks). Home telephone services and facsimile services such as home (personal) communications are provided by these public communications networks and so are business communications services to a certain extent.

It is desirable that public communications networks be operated and managed by one or more enterprises in order to satisfy the following objectives:

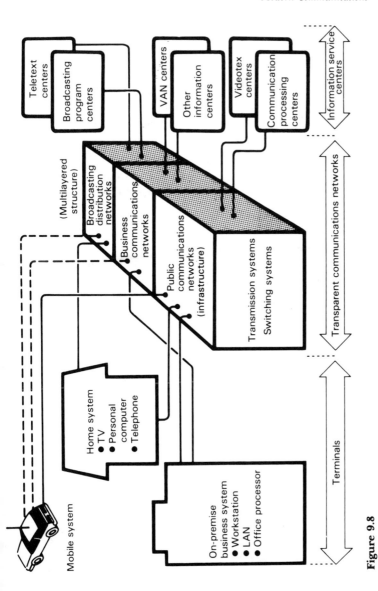

Figure 9.8
Combination of multilayered structure of transparent communication
networks and terminals/information service centers

- To provide good quality, uniform services on a nationwide basis.

- To have the capability to respond quickly to abnormal traffic concentrations due to disasters or social phenomena.

- To have surplus reserves for research and development, and to keep expanding facilities in order to improve the infrastructure in the future.

- To have adaptable and mobile personnel and service facilities for network operation and maintenance in remote locations.

Business Communications Networks Layer

Communications networks operated by private enterprises for profit connect specific information sources and destinations. Business is conducted only in the areas or fields that private companies find profitable. By using company-owned private switching networks, leasing part of the public communications network, or operating communications facilities used on an on-demand basis, businesses can save on intracorporate communications expenses and further, when possible, on rental income earned from other businesses using their communications facilities. On-demand use refers to using services as they are required. Communications services provided by these private networks include telephones, telexes, and facsimiles, as well as data communication through various combinations of computers or data processing terminals.

In value-added network (VAN) services incorporating computer systems at information services centers, business communications may expand to those between different enterprises in related fields. In these cases transfer/switching functions of public communications networks may be used in the transfer routes. Leased line services for wide area transfer and intelligent electronic private branch exchanges (IEPBX) for switching functions may also be utilized. In plants and offices some on-premise networks may use IEPBX or local area networks (LAN). These are all included in private facilities for business use.

Businesses often base their communications operations on one means of transfer, such as satellite communications, or a specific information service, such as the shared information services of electronic mail and videotex. The concept of businesses earning income for offering specific information services, particularly automatic large-scale computer services, is original for value-added communications networks (VAN). The VAN business does not necessarily aim at uniform nationwide services. As emphasis is placed on pursuing income from communications in the business communications network layer that includes VANs, the distinction between public communications networks and VANs may be gradually lessened.

Broadcasting Distribution Networks

Broadcasting distribution networks may be distinguished from public and business communications networks by their unidirectional, one-to-many, network flow. As shown in figures 9.5 and 9.6, in the distribution of programs between broadcasting program centers and local broadcasting stations, parts of public communications networks or the broadcasting company's own distribution networks (including broadcasting distribution satellite systems) can be used. Radio and TV programs are now distributed independently of user access systems via terrestrial broadcasting, CATV cable networks, or direct broadcasting satellites (DBS).

There are yet other considerations besides the multilayered structures I have described: for example, the different circuit-switching networks, packet-switching networks, and leased lines in public communications networks; simultaneous networks operated by several companies in business communications networks; and simultaneous numerous broadcasting channels in broadcasting services that form part of home communications. How such networks are employed may depend on the different technology and managerial practices of the organization operating the communications facilities.

Although I have attempted to treat public, business, and broadcast networks as contributing equally to a multilayered structure of communications, I would like to emphasize that the public communications network layer is the most important one, and because it constitutes a national infrastructure, it must maintain its integrity and nationwide service capacity.

New electronic media now being planned cover all of the three fields—public, business, and home systems. In the development of these new electronic media, I believe that it is necessary to consider each of the functions equally and comprehensively in terms of the concept of the multilayered structure of communications.

10

Components of Modern Communications Systems

Home Systems

Although C&C technology has begun to be used in homes, it is still difficult to visualize clearly the shape it will take in the future. However, the need for home systems will be realized quickly, and these systems will surely become popular. This is partly because humankind has always sought high-quality information as well as the ability to communicate over wide areas and partly because advanced countries have already begun to enter the information society.

To begin with, until the first half of this century the only widespread communications media that existed were telephones (a point-to-point bidirectional medium) and radio broadcasting (a point-to-plane or one-to-many unidirectional medium). From the audio/video mass media age in the latter half of this century, represented by television broadcasting, we are moving toward the home information era. What lets us foresee this directly is the explosive growth in the use of personal computers in developed countries. Home markets represent the bottom of C&C system markets; they are fascinatingly diverse and have infinite possibilities. Let us consider some of the needs of information handled by home systems:

1. *More variety in information for entertainment* The extensive need for entertainment at homes, which are primarily places

of relaxation, has been proved by the high popularity of television. Today, with life-styles becoming more diverse and entertainment preferences more individualized and expanded to include higher-quality video and audio, people are seeking more freedom in program selection and reception time.

2. *More variety in information for daily living*   Every day people receive the news, weather forecasts, economic statistics, regional information, and information on crimes and disasters. Highlights of the news were conventionally obtained from TV and radio, and more detailed, accumulated information from newspapers and magazines. It is expected that from now on these media will offer a wider choice of contents and reception times.

3. *Telehandling of daily activities*   In the past it was necessary to go outside the home to shop, withdraw money from the bank, handle various procedures at government and municipal agencies, reserve hotels or transportation, receive medical treatment, and manage one's health. There is a potential desire to do each of these at home on one's free time, or to secure the safety of one's home during an absence. It is greatly expected that each of these functions can be performed using the new electronic media.

4. *Expectations for telecommuting*   From the standpoint of saving commuting time and transportation costs and energy, liberalizing living patterns, and increasing employment opportunities for homemakers, the aged, and physically handicapped people, greater use of telecommuting is expected. The savings in time and energy will be huge. Moreover productivity will increase because people will be released from time constraints and will be able to work during their most efficient time of day. In creative jobs the effects will be particularly pronounced. For mothers with young children, child care and work will become compatible. Home shopping and home banking, which will be described in the home life subsystem, will promote timesavings.

Although some disadvantages have been brought up, such as lack of face-to-face communication and hindrances deriving from inadequate housing conditions in Japan, telecommuting will continue to grow with such support facilities as satellite offices, office malls incorporating many satellite offices, and the adoption of flexible commuting schedules.

It will be convenient to be able to work, to receive medical diagnoses, to shop, and to make banking transactions at home. However, there is the danger of a simple mistake causing big trouble. It is therefore necessary to prevent troubles from occurring by taking double or triple confirmation procedures during operation. Moreover it is a matter of course that systems will have to be perfected to ensure absolute protection of privacy.

C&C Home System Image

Future homes will be equipped with central home computers, which will be supplemented with terminals for various service media or home media terminals that incorporate all media services, and a home network (home bus) that connects the terminals with each other. This system comprises three functional subsystems: home control, home living, and work at home. Figure 10.1 shows in more detail the contents of the home systems shown in figures 9.5 and 9.6.

The home control subsystem will monitor each part of the house, control air conditioners, open or close windows, doors, gates, and garage doors, control switching between commercial power supply and solar cell power, and warn of abnormal conditions of electric power and gas. These functions will make our homes safer, more convenient, and more comfortable.

The home life subsystem will be used to enrich lives by widening cultural contacts. People will be able to enjoy a rich variety of entertainment services in the information society and have more leisure time in which to do it because time-consuming day-to-day tasks will be done through the computer. Various information service media that can be received at home are now being planned. These can be classified by communications mode as the unidirectional or bidirectional type.

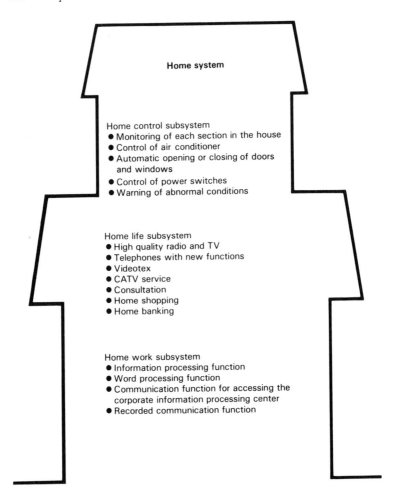

Figure 10.1
A possible home system

Unidirectional service is represented by conventional radio/ TV broadcasting. High-definition TV (HDTV) and larger screens will greatly enhance TV viewing, especially in live coverage of sports events and theatrical performances. Bidirectional service is the most desirable form of information service, for it provides the services desired by users on request at their desired time.

The most popular bidirectional service is the telephone. With the videotex and bidirectional CATV service, study, medical consultation, travel consultation, reservation of hotels/airplanes, and shopping and banking at home will all become possible.

Home work subsystems will make possible telecommuting and provide information processing functions, word processing functions, communication functions to access various shared-type information service centers, and record communication functions by facsimile. Since with this system people will be able to apportion some of their office work to their homes, it may be thought of as a kind of remote office automation (OA) system.

Home Systems and Their Service Trends

To enjoy the variety of services home systems can offer, it is necessary to develop the appropriate structures for them. It may be easier to envision the connections between home systems and the service media by considering them as basic services and extended services, as shown in figure 10.2.

The left half of this illustration shows the basic services, which are already partially in place. The right half shows the arrangement of equipment and functions that will provide extended services in the future. Present-day home system equipment comprises telephones, TV and radio receivers, and personal computers. In the future these will be integrated into various home media terminals, each of which will include specific functions. Among these, home computers will have the functions of processing/conversion, and storage and retrieval of the information that enters, leaves, or is generated in the home. They

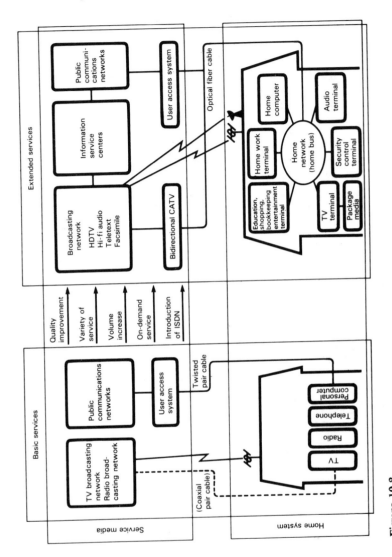

Figure 10.2
Trend in home systems and services

will also function as word processors. The home computer, which will advance to a type more suitable for home needs than the present personal computer, will also serve as the center for home control and home security.

As described before, because various terminal equipment will be installed in homes, it will become necessary to build home networks (home buses) for systematizing mutual connections among those terminals. The coaxial cable is sufficient for home networks at present, but optical fibers will be mainly used in the future. However, because the home is the place for relaxation, and particularly because untrained people should be able to use the equipment easily, it is not appropriate to transplant OA terminal equipment in its present form. It is necessary that these terminals be made suitable for the home in function, operation, and design.

From this viewpoint home terminals, which will combine audio equipment, a TV, VCR, and personal computer, will be divided into four categories: for use by business people for telecommuting at home, for use by homemakers for processing household matters, for use by children for education, and for use by aged people who prefer ease of operation, watching, and listening. An example is shown in figure 9.6.

Access Systems for Home Systems

The access systems that are necessary before the various home services can be used are shown in figure 10.3. This figure was prepared by arranging the access systems for home systems shown in figures 9.5, 9.6, 9.7, 10.1, and 10.2 according to their practical applications.

Further progress in the direct broadcasting system (DBS), which is included in the broadcasting system, is expected; this will make high-quality TV possible. CATV systems in the broadcasting system now mainly use coaxial cables, but optical fibers will predominate in the future because of their dual advantages of wide bandwidth and economy.

Types of access systems			Time frame Present	Future
Broadcasting systems	Radio system (No. 1)		MF/HF (radio) VHF/UHF (TV)	
		Direct broadcasting satellite system (DBS)	SHF	
	Wired system	CATV system	Coaxial pair cable	Optical fiber cable (Integrated Services Digital Network: ISDN)
User access systems		Public communication system for subscribers	Mainly copper twisted pair cable	
	Radio system (No. 2)	Access system for mobile subcribers	UHF automobile telephone	
	Package system		Tape recorder VCR Audio disk Video disk	Digital audio disk (recordable) Digital video disk (recordable)

Figure 10.3
Home access systems

In contrast, in the wired systems of the user access system, a pair of copper-twisted cables is now mainly used for analog-type telephone communications. However, the integrated services digital network (ISDN) type of subscriber access system is being studied in CCITT. CCITT recommends that the interface at the standard transmission rate be used on the premise of the transmission of two-channel bidirectional 64 kilobits per second (so-called B channel) and one-channel 16 kilobits per second (so-called D channel), or "2B plus D" on the same wire. If this is put into practical use, the capacity of the circuits connecting the public communications network and the home network (home buses) described earlier will be much larger than that of the conventional analog-type interface. With this, the applications of C&C at home can be expected to advance greatly.

Moreover, as demand increases for image services and higher-speed information transmission, it will become necessary to make the bandwidth of the subscriber system connected to the public communications network much wider. For this purpose optical fiber cables will be gradually introduced in the subscriber system.

The broadcasting system services and the public communications system services have been planned and developed separately up to now. However, it will be possible for both services to share one optical cable when connected to the home, which will make it possible to integrate the access system.

The mobile subscriber access system shown in the figure 10.3 as a radio system for the user access system is not a home system in the strict sense. However, it may be considered to be the extension of the home system, which is why it is included in the figure. At present the mobile telephone is in actual use, and it may not be long before the equipment is extremely miniaturized and integrated into a wristwatch.

Next, there is the packaged information supply system such as tapes and disks—these may be more appropriately called a kind of information media itself rather than access systems. Information packages will be used mainly for entertainment and education, particularly in fields where real-time presentation is not required. This is the access system characterized by a kind of material flow where information packages are treated as physical matter to be conveyed.

Digitalization of audio tape recorders and VCRs has greatly improved the quality of reproduced sounds and pictures. Also video cameras incorporating VCRs have been further miniaturized. This high-quality audio/video equipment will gradually find wider usage together with the practical application of direct broadcasting satellite systems. As described here, the future of the home systems seems rosy, indeed. However, for it to be fully realized, the following three key factors will be important:

- The service supply system established must be capable of grasping the needs of users and responding to them promptly.
- Workstations must be easy to use and must fit the home environment.
- The costs for equipment and services must be reasonable.

Business Communications

The office automation (OA) system supports information activities in the office by C&C technology. When conventional office communication means such as telephones are included, the OA system may be considered comprehensively as a modern business communications system.

Here I will outline the basic structure of the OA system as it relates to the standard office system. Intrapremises communications networks (LAN in a general sense) and wide area networks (WAN) may be positioned as basic elements of this system.

Basic Structure of the Office System in a Single Office/ Plant

Figure 10.4 shows the conceptual connection of various office system equipment and terminals to intrapremise communications networks—namely the local area network (LAN) which is

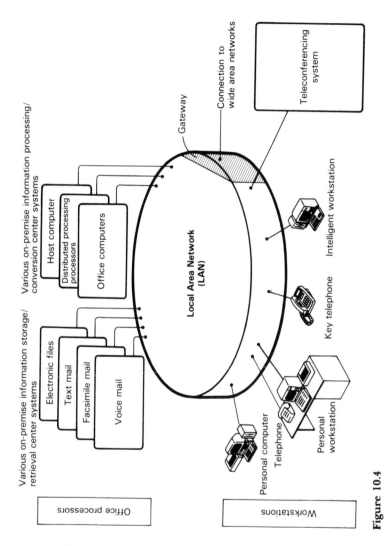

Figure 10.4
LAN and various office automation subsystems

seen at the center. This office system includes various subsystems that can be classified by function into three constituent elements:

- workstations (WS),
- local area networks (LAN),
- office processors (OP).

First, the workstation is the general term for the various terminals shown at the bottom of the illustration. Figure 10.5 presents an example of a basic functional block. The workstation shown in the figure is representative of the future multifunctional type of workstation which is equipped with several kinds of human interfaces. These workstations should ideally be small and designed in such a way that they can be installed easily on or beside desks in the office and be easy to use.

Various present-day communications terminals such as telephones, key telephone sets, facsimile terminals, and teletex terminals can be regarded as workstations having the classical voice-type interface. The workstation shown in figure 10.5, by having its own processor and suitable memory as intelligent functions, makes it possible for office workers to perform the functions of information processing/conversion and storage at their desks. For a single independent workstation it has considerable ability. Personal computers and word processors are examples of this type of workstation.

As shown in the figure such workstations are equipped with a network interface port through which connections are made to the local area network (LAN) and further to the wide area network (WAN). They can therefore serve in two fundamental capacities. First, they enable business communications between office workers to proceed smoothly. Also they will make it possible for various electronic message and mail services to be introduced in the office in order to transfer business communications both timewise and spacewise. Second, when these workstations are connected through a LAN to large-, medium-, or small-size computers having high-level arithmetic functions, high-level document processing function, or large-capacity in-

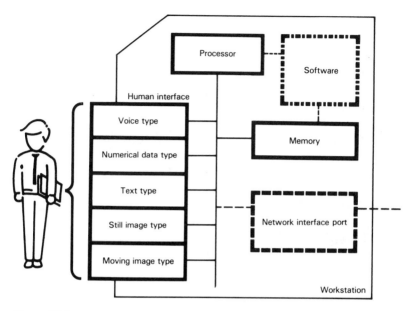

Figure 10.5
General form of the multifunctional workstation

formation storage functions, they can utilize intelligent functions that the single independent workstation cannot economically include. It will also become possible to share the use of database services and electronic file services.

Figure 10.6 shows how an office system would be planned for a single floor, and figure 10.7 gives the plan for the entire building. "Office processor" is the general term used for various shared-type high-level information processing/storage facilities. The office processors in figures 10.6 and 10.7 are divided into the small- and large-scale office processors. It may be a wise practice to arrange hierarchically shared-type facilities and facilities of different intelligence levels in accordance with sizes of offices or plants and their organizational and hierarchical positions.

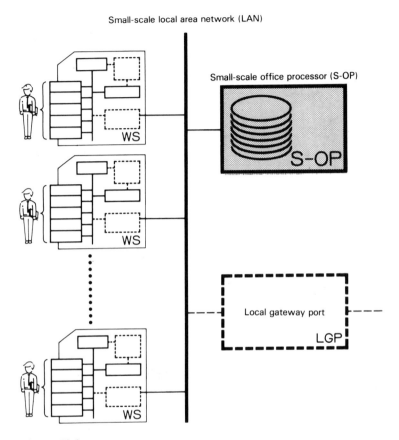

Figure 10.6
Plan of office system for a single floor

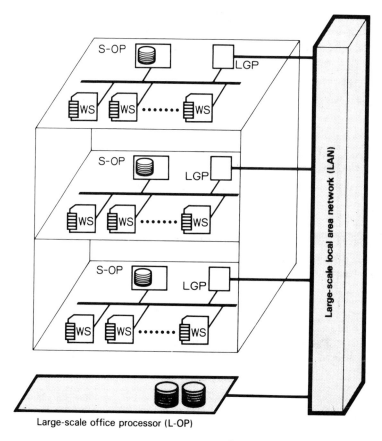

Large-scale office processor (L-OP)

Figure 10.7
Plan of office system for an entire building

Basic Structure of the Office System Connected to WANs

In large corporations an office system must extend to satellite offices or plants. The same workstation as described for the single office/plant may be used, but the local area networks (LAN) must be extended from intrapremises networks to interpremises networks to form a wide area network (WAN) interconnecting LANs. This is quite similar to the structure of the corporate communications system today. In accordance with the expanded office system facilities, there may be hierarchical expansion of intelligent ability for the office processor. Figure 10.8 shows the basic structure of an intracorporate office system that extends to several offices or plants. The wide area network has two layers: the business communications networks layer and the public communications networks layer.

It may be possible to consider an office system that is extended to serve as a public information service center (for example, a public data bank or computation center) that is located externally, as shown in figure 10.9. There is, however, more hierarchy to be considered in this case.

By looking at figures 10.5 through 10.9, you can understand that a hierarchy of information processing/storage functions in the office system (workstations, small-, large-, or corporate-size office processors, and external information service centers) exists, that there are two kinds of network facilities—the local area networks (LAN) and the wide area networks (WAN)—and that the interrelationships between information processing/storage functions and the networking (information transferring) functions are very essential. Thus you can imagine the various office activities being conducted by office workers through human interfaces at workstations.

The General Structure of the Office System

The three constituent elements of an office system in a single office or on plant premises are shown in figure 10.10 and may be denoted as follows:

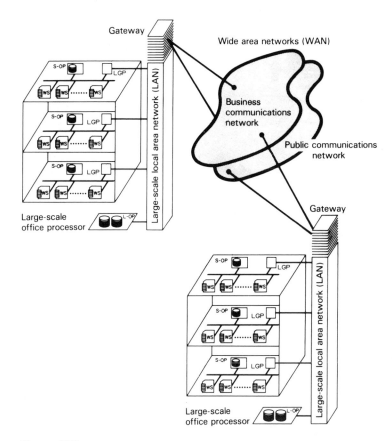

Figure 10.8
Intracorporate office system covering multiple offices and plants

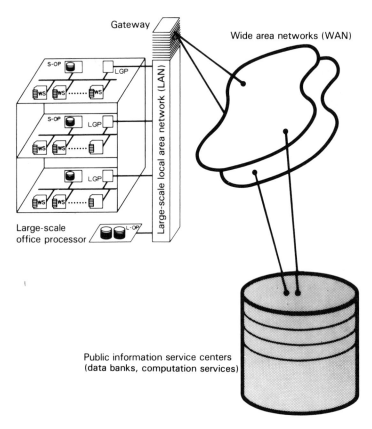

Figure 10.9
Office system connected to system connected to external information service

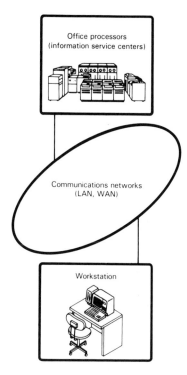

Figure 10.10
General composition of office system

- Workstations which generally involve any type of human interface and are located near and operated by professionals or office workers.

- Communications networks covering both local area networks and wide area networks.

- Office processors arranged functionally, geographically, or hierarchically, inside or outside a business organization.

Figure 10.11 shows how an office system would accommodate functional, geographical, and hierarchical expansion. By comparing figures 10.10 and 10.11 with figures 9.7 and 9.8, you can see that these business and office systems represent one feature of modern communications systems.

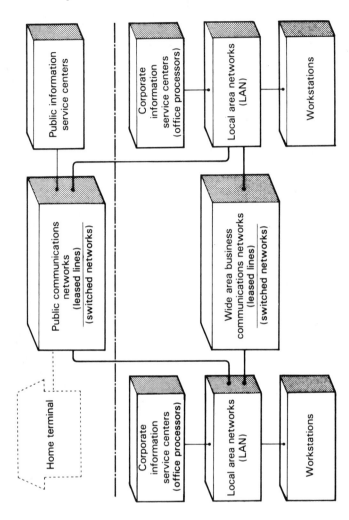

Figure 10.11
General model for office system extending to multiple offices and plants

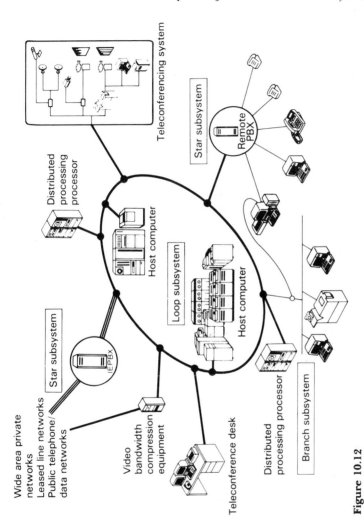

Wide area private
networks
Leased line networks
Public telephone/
data networks

Star subsystem

EPBX

Video
bandwidth
compression
equipment

Teleconference desk

Distributed
processing
processor

Host computer

Loop subsystem

Host computer

Distributed
processing processor

Branch subsystem

Teleconferencing system

Star subsystem

Remote
PBX

Figure 10.12
Layout of various terminals/workstations and equipment for office
systems via C&C optical network system

Actual Composition of LAN and WAN

Figure 10.12 shows an actual example of LAN whose general arrangement of three intrapremise network subsystems (star, loop, and branch) represents NEC's C&C NET model. This model consists of a local area network that includes a star network that has an intelligent electronic private branch exchange system (shown as IEPBX and remote PBX in figure 10.12) as the hub of the star subsystem. Such an arrangement may also be considered for an office system set up in a single office or plant.

Figure 10.13 adapts the detailed structural model of local and wide area networks to a corporate office system connecting a great number of offices or plants. The satellite communications system portion, which is shown separately in the wide area network, is also highlighted, although it is functionally incorporated and operated as part of the public and business communications networks. The metropolitan area network (MAN) portion shows various alternative systems separately from the wide area network. Although the wide area network portion is drawn as one domestic network, it may actually exist as a combination of international and domestic networks. Also integrated services digital networks (ISDN), which are being studied by CCITT, will be included in the future image of the wide area network.

Mobile Communications Services

Mobile Communications in the Information Society

Mobile communications will play an important role as an interface between humans and systems in C&C systems, enabling individuals to have access to information systems at any place and time using terminals located nearby.

As shown in figures 9.6 and 9.8, mobile communications technology has been indispensable in maintaining communications with mobile vehicles such as automobiles and ships. Mobile communications is expected to progress even further in the future, providing the means for more comfortable and

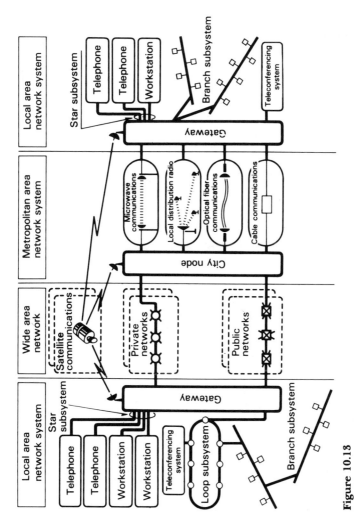

Figure 10.13

Structural model for LAN and WAN in office system connecting multiple offices and plants

freer interface between humans and systems at various information terminals. This makes mobile communications an important element of modern communications.

There are some points we have to consider in having the means to communicate on a "whenever, wherever, and with whomever" basis. A significant accomplishment will be that desired information may be obtained at any time because communications facilities will have been widely installed. Today information may be transmitted to a place or at a time that is not convenient; the conventional telephone service is oriented to on-demand immediate conversation initiated by the caller. However, in future communications selection and storage functions that both send and receive information at each party's convenience would have higher priority. This feature will be particularly important in mobile communications.

Technical Background of Mobile Communications

Transmission media that enable communications to take place with mobile vehicles are radio, light, and ultrasonic waves. Of these, radio waves have been used mainly because of their excellent propagation characteristics. Nevertheless, radio waves are limited resources that require international agreements on their use. Since the demand for radio waves is increasing, it is important to develop technologies for the efficient use of frequency resources and to utilize new frequency bands. For communications within limited areas, the use of light and ultrasonic waves will certainly be pursued in the future.

Representative methods for using radio frequencies efficiently include the small-zone cellular system and the multichannel access system, which are now actually being used for mobile telephone systems. The small-zone system is characterized by many radio base stations with the same frequency being used at somewhat distant locations. Supposing that the number of mobile stations that can be accommodated by one base station is constant, the total number of mobile stations the system can accommodate increases in proportion to the installation density of the base stations. In the multichannel access system there are a number of channels being shared by many stations. This system is also used in multichannel access radios (MCA), trunked dispatch systems, and personal radio telephones. These systems are expected to progress further in the future as technology to increase efficiency in frequency resource usage is developed.

Looking at the small-zone system from a different perspective, it is based on the concept of covering as much area as possible by wired fixed-point communications, limiting the use of radio waves to short-distance communications. This system may be the best for saving frequency resources in crowded areas where radio waves are highly needed, although these needs must be balanced with economic considerations. Conversely, in scarcely populated areas where radio waves are less needed, it may be more cost-effective to use wireless fixed-point communications or mobile communications in place of wired fixed-point communications.

Another method for saving frequency resources is to reduce redundancy in the information to be transferred. This can be made possible by upgrading communication processing at the terminal. Methods include paying attention only to the changed portions of information against time in data transmission, or using bandwidth compression technologies now being developed in various ways for image and voice transmission.

Particularly for voice, it will be possible to realize large savings in frequency resources by using voice-recognition methods based on digital technology, which is expected to progress significantly in the future. It will be also necessary to consider fully not only voice but also nonvoice messages, like telegrams, as personal information transfer media. Replacement of voice by messages and quick transfer by packet transmission technology will realize not only frequency resource savings but also energy savings in mobile terminals.

It is required that full consideration be given to the input/output operation of the mobile terminal, which must provide unrestricted, comfortable human interface, from the viewpoints of software, hardware, and human engineering. Although miniaturization and light weight of mobile terminals have been largely attained, future progress will depend on the advance in LSIs. When considering a mobile radio terminal as small as a credit card, the most difficult task will be to develop a correspondingly small and high-energy density power source.

Various Mobile Communications Services

The interface between humans and communications networks in mobile communications can be realized on various levels, as shown in figure 10.14. At point A is an example of direct access to the international communications networks. INMARSAT and AEROSAT are satellite communications systems for vehicles moving around the world, such as oceangoing ships and aircraft. However, AEROSAT is still in the developmental stage, so these services must depend on radio communications. The sea rescue system is another global network that takes advantage of the characteristics of radio communications.

At point B appear automobile telephone systems, cordless telephone systems, and radio-paging service systems; these machines constitute the subscriber access system in the public communications networks. As public communications networks are digitalized and services are integrated, these devices will handle various information media. The realization of portable pocket telephones and credit card size terminals will provide further personalization of communications.

While such systems are saving frequency resources, they are also expected to increase greatly the number of subscribers that can be accommodated. As individuals acquire more than one terminal, individual person-assigned and terminal-assigned numbering will need to be managed and operated in an integrated manner. Also, because of the mobility of public mobile communications such as automobile telephones, future concerns will center on establishing global standards and numbering plans.

Point C shows the means of interface between humans and networks in business and home networks. Included in these are

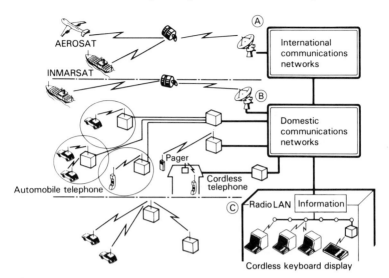

Figure 10.14
Communications networks and mobile communications technologies

cordless information terminals in the office; remotely controlled robots in plants; multichannel access (MCA) radio systems and radio position detection systems in cities; various remote control, remote sensing systems for security; and cordless telephones and intercoms in homes.

Some of these are used as single units, but it will become possible for them to be interconnected with and operated through various centers dispersed widely through public communications networks. Besides the foregoing, office-use information terminals and futuristic remote input/output units with high processing ability will allow operators to position themselves anywhere within several meters of the units.

Thus, as unused frequency bands are exploited and the technology to use frequencies effectively progresses, mobile communications technology will connect humans with C&C more closely by improving work efficiency and the workplace environment and by bringing a more comfortable life to the home.

Positioning of VAN

Now let us collectively consider value-added networks—that is, what has recently been called the VAN system in Japan—which can be positioned in relation to the overall and partial images of modern communications explained so far. We will consider VAN from a somewhat technical angle, and in addition we will need to pay attention to its impact on social and economical structures that are related to the contents of information flow.

VAN is, as the name implies, the network that provides some added value, not simply information transfer. As described earlier, a feature of modern communications is that it combines information processing and storage with conventional information transfer. Since information processing and storage can be regarded as the basic functions of producing added value, various VANs will be incorporated in the total modern communications system. In this section, let us focus our attention on the VAN in relation to data communications.

The following are somewhat more concrete examples of added value produced by information processing and storage:

1. *Added value by information processing*
   • Added value to express as data human intentions that can be handled by data communications.
   • Added value to analyze and recognize the contents of data.
   • Added value to present necessary data in desired form.

2. *Added value by information storage*
   • Added value to select only necessary data from among numerous pieces of information.
   • Added value to take out necessary data at the required time.

A combination of these added values will produce even larger added value. Such added value is naturally combined with the normal information transfer functions of delivering information to remotely located recipients. In other words, unlike leased line services that simply transfer information in the form of data or switching services that simply connect terminals, value-added services of VANs include communications processing services such as data conversion and storage offered through intelligent functions that are arranged in the networks. In this case communications processing is defined as partial information processing which is conducted without changing the essential contents of the communicated information so that effective communications can be performed between various remotely located data communications service functions. There are four main functions:

• Adjustment of communication speeds, compensation for differences in internal codes, and adjustment of communications protocol between equipment connected to the network; all are processed at the relay node in the network.

• Broadcasting function to send the same data to more than one recipient.

• Conversion of formats into business forms such as vouchers.

• Media conversion from coded information to image information, or vice versa.

These functions, which center on communications processing, may be included in the end users' facilities which are connected to the transparent communications networks shown in figures 9.5 and 9.6.

Still, value may be added by information processing services, such as remote computing and database access services. There may further be value added by long-term information storage services (archival file services). These service functions can be provided by information service centers, office processors in local business systems, and intelligent terminals or workstations (refer to figures 9.5 to 9.8 and 10.4 to 10.10).

Addition of value by information processing services covers remote computing services and database services to many unspecified users or services that offer total business operations for single industries or groups of specific industries. In the latter case information processing, transfer, and storage are executed as a complete business work package. A network such as this is the business-oriented VAN. In this regard the detailed classification of what has recently been called VAN in Japan can be extended to include service operation mode, purpose, and specific industry service point of views.

Classification by Service Operation Mode

The VAN service operation can be a self-operation or a service provider dependent type. The self-operation type may get into VAN in any of the following ways:

• as a natural result of business activity,

• as a natural result of a spinoff policy,

• through a decision to pursue new business opportunities within the limits of cooperation within an industry or even by linking several industries.

Among the reasons for adopting the VAN service provider dependent type may be to reduce risk by eliminating the substantial initial investment and to supplement lack of know-how by utilizing specialized vendors.

Classification of VAN by Purpose

There are various services promoted by VAN, whose purposes may best be illustrated by the following diagram:

```
┌Circuit charge reduction type
│
└Value-added type in
   the original sense┬General purpose service type
                     │
                     ├Specific industry service type┬Own business
                     │                               │efficiency
                     │                               │improve-
                     │                               │ment type
                     │                               │
                     │                               ├Intraindustry
                     │                               │cooperation
                     │                               │(horizontal)
                     │                               │type
                     │                               │
                     │                               └Interindustry
                     │                                cooperation
                     │                                (vertical) type
                     │
                     └Equipment/software sales business
                      tie-up type
```

The first case in the circuit charge reduction type system aims at taking advantage of the communications network service providers' circuit charge system of offering larger capacity circuits at reduced charge. The second case is to reduce cost by collecting many low-speed circuit users and bundling them together. Naturally the benefit of introducing this type of service is that it depends heavily on the circuit charge system. Because this type of service is one of reselling circuits only, it is difficult to maintain the loyality of users. Since the fundamental information processing and storage functions are not included, the circuit charge reduction type VAN is considered technically to be at the very first stage, though it is also called a VAN system commercially.

The value-added type in the original sense can be divided into three services. The first, the general purpose service type, is the name for the service offered to many unspecified users by information service centers connected to the network. Conventional remote computing services (RCS) are included in this category.

The specific industry service type was explained previously as the business-oriented VAN. This is further divided into three types. Among them, the own business efficiency improvement type is spontaneously developed into a VAN as the efficiencies of affiliated corporations are expanded, taking advantage of deregulation related to communications. It should be left to the parties concerned whether this should be recognized as a VAN or as the natural expansion of an on-line system.

If these are treated as a VAN, they may form the mainstream of the market for the time being. The interindustry cooperation type aims at expanding the quantity and scope of operations, that is, the size of the business pie, by interconnecting similar networks constructed and run by different corporations. A typical example can be seen in the financial industry. By contrast, the interindustry cooperation type aims at improving a company's own business efficiency and at completing its networks by involving related corporations in different businesses. The objective here is to gain an advantage over other companies in the same industry. Various plans are being forwarded centering on the manufacturing industry or the distribution business.

In the equipment/software sales business tie-up type VAN service, suppliers not only sell equipment and software to customers but also offer services that can be provided by equipment and software. This will enable customers to obtain the fourth option of getting services in addition to purchase, rental, and lease. This type of business will be effective in providing backup services, processing of traffic overflow during peaks, and temporary substitution in case of upgrading, for the same equipment and software can be used as if purchased.

Any one of these VANs may be useful, but the key to success in the VAN service business will be to decide on the best mix of VAN services to be provided by giving due consideration to all the types of VANs outlined here.

Classification of Specific Industry Service Type VANs from the Added Value Viewpoint

Specific industry service type VANs may be roughly classified into the following three categories:

• pure information-flow-oriented type VAN,

• material-flow-oriented type VAN,

• finance-oriented type VAN.

The pure information-flow-oriented type VAN provides communications services for information in the distribution industry, including retailers and department stores, at the time commodities are ordered and shipped. The material-flow-oriented type VAN handles information accompanying the flow of materials and commodities and provides information services at the shipment and arrival of commodities to customers in the trucking and marine transport industries. The finance-oriented type VAN handles information accompanying the flow of money and provides services regarding the flow of money and is related to both the pure information-flow-oriented type VAN and the material-flow-oriented type VAN.

These VANs of course include communications processing such as the format conversion described earlier. These VANs are not only utilized independently but also can be connected organically to other networks. A VAN comprising various specific industry service type VANs that are interconnected to each other may be called an integrated system VAN.

Moreover this type of VAN was used in a limited area in the connected form at the beginning and then developed from the regional to the national level, with regional VANs being combined further and covering areas as extensive as a wide area VAN. Further some VANs of this type have become multinational in size, and they provide services as an advanced added value network that allows customers, for example, to purchase foreign products more effectively.

Refer now to figure 10.15, where the logical and geographical structures of Japanese nationwide VAN systems are presented for hardware in the form of layered maps. The top group consists of VAN information service center allocation planes. Each plane of this group indicates the allocation of various VAN centers (large-scale computer centers and relatively small-size computer subcenters) that belong to different VAN systems (or VAN service providers). Each plane represents different VAN systems that can be specified from the service function point of view (for example, horizontal/vertical specific industry service type VAN). Information service centers (computer centers in this case) on the same plane are of course functionally interworking via one or several transparent transfer network installation planes, which are illustrated as the middle group in figure 10.15. The network planes can be distinguished by operation organization (enterprises) and/or by operation mode (fixed connected/circuit switched/packet switched). For example, transparent network A can correspond solely to the VAN centers of system II. Also network B can be shared by systems II, III, and IV.

The bottom group of figure 10.15 is composed of maps that illustrate the deployment of individual VAN users' workstations

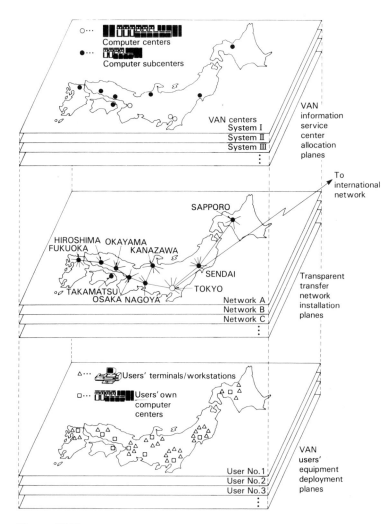

Figure 10.15
Envisioned logic for nationwide VAN systems in Japan

or intelligent terminals and/or the users' own host computers which provide various service applications. The terminals can be dispersed throughout the region or installed in clusters in office buildings. In the latter case they are usually connected by LANs, together with corresponding office processors at the users' computer centers.

Hypothetically, for user 1 to receive VAN services of some kind, he or she can access, say, VAN system I via corresponding network A. Users 2 through 4 can access commonly to, say, VAN system V via network I. The Japanese nationwide VAN system VIII can interconnect with VAN centers in foreign countries via the international gateway of the network that accesses the global transparent network. These are just some of the many installation and utilization patterns possible for VAN systems.

If the structure of figure 10.15 is compared with those of modern communications systems shown in figures 9.5 and 9.8, it can be seen that the top, middle, and bottom groups of figure 10.15 correspond to some parts of the information service centers, transparent communications networks, and terminals generally presented in those figures.

In the information service centers that provide information processing services many powerful processing (conversion) and storage (filing) functions are applied based on state-of-the-art computer hardware/software technologies. Moreover the information is handled in various information media forms such as voice, data, text, and images. Information service centers may be generally considered to be those for value-added functions in VAN. VAN in a broad sense may also be called an advanced intelligent network.

The automatic interpretation telephone system to be described in the next chapter is a good example of one such advanced value-added system. In the future the functions of computer-based information service centers will greatly expand, and there will be a variety of value-added application functions.

New Electronic Media

We have examined so far modern communications systems concentrating on electrical (electronic and optical) information handling. However, if we look at communications systems from the standpoint of general societal activities, there are other fields, such as print journalism and the postal service that have existed much longer than electrical communications. Information in these fields, though not necessarily in form of electrical signals, is transferred and stored in the form of text or pictures printed or written on paper. Figure 10.16 shows the relationship between the nonelectrical and electrical information media systems. The three boxes in each system correspond to terminals, transfer networks, and information service centers.

In the future in advanced countries all economic activities and corresponding value addition will be moved and controlled by information handling (processing/communications). This will create the so-called "information network society." This information network may be equivalent to the modern communications system. One aspect of modern communications is that information handled by conventional nonelectrical information media will eventually be handled by the electronic media. This may be regarded as one side of the development of modern communications.

These new electronic media, if arranged by function, can be classified into three categories, as shown in figure 10.17: package system-type media, transfer network system-type media, and information processing/providing system-type media. These three categories relate to the three elements of C&C information handling: information generation, transfer, and storage.

Package system-type media refers only to memory and individual generation of information by end users. The feature of this system is that information used at users' terminals is transported as material flow in the form of a portable information package. Home computers (personal computers) for use by individuals may be regarded as one item of this classification.

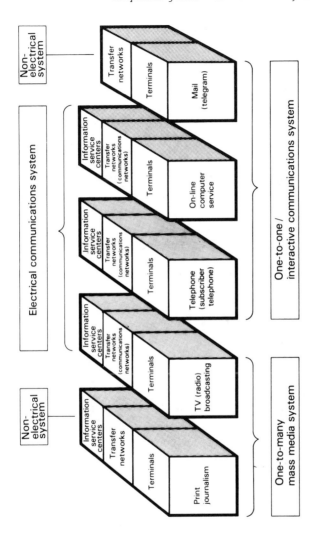

Figure 10.16
Classification of existing electrical and nonelectrical information media systems

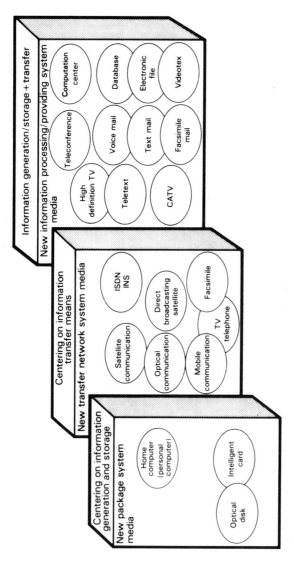

Figure 10.17
New media groups combining information generation, storage and transfer functions

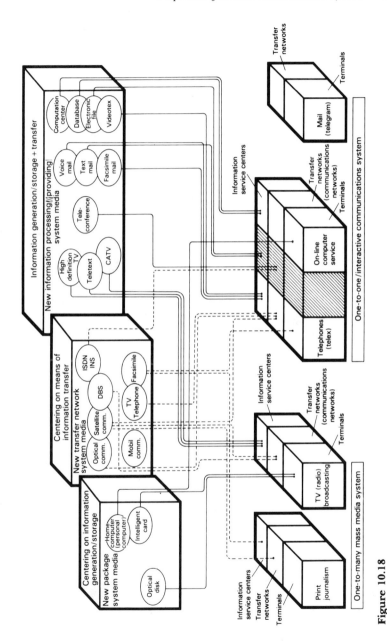

Figure 10.18
Relationship between new media groups and the entire modern communications system

It is necessary to keep in mind that together with TV receivers and telephones, home computers will eventually become one of the key information terminals for future C&C systems.

Transfer network system-type media provide new functions and great economy for point-to-point systems (public communications including conventional telephones) and point-to-multiple points systems (broadcasting systems), or bidirectional electrical communication media. The integrated services digital network (ISDN) and the information network system (ISN) proposed by the NTT Corporation are two such systems related to the expansion of the telephone system. Further, satellite communications is being applied to telephone communications networks, computer communications networks, and image communications networks. The direct broadcasting satellite system (DBS) is a new means of distributing programs directly to viewers. Optical communications systems, TV telephone systems, and mobile communications systems are related media centering on information transfer.

Information processing/providing system-type media relates to the new capabilities of various information service centers, including VANs, to serve as facilities for shared-type information generation and storage. These transmit and receive information to and from users' terminals via information transfer functions. Computation centers and databases are positioned as shared-type information processing/storage facilities related to VANs.

Figure 10.18 illustrates how these new media relate to various parts of the modern communications system. If we compare the bottom half of this illustration with figure 10.16, we see how electrical communications in the existing media has developed into the modern communications system. For example, the telephone system is connected with the on-line computer service system as shown by the shaded area in figure 10.18. This indicates that conventional telephone services and computerized communication services are being functionally integrated, joining in parallel terminals, transfer networks, and information service centers as advancements occur in C&C technologies.

11

Construction of Global Infrastructure

In chapters 9 and 10 I have arranged and shown the overall composition of modern communications systems as well as details of various contributing elements as they relate to the infrastructure of the information network society. It may be possible to promote the construction of a global infrastructure as one of the strategic policies of this modern communications system concept. The purpose of such a plan will be to emphasize the realization of global modern communications as promptly as possible from the very beginning.

The communications systems we have today were established to make it possible to see, listen to, or talk with any other person at any time and place. It is very desirable for the peaceful development of human society to try to achieve this on a global scale, irrespective of national boundaries. In this chapter I will outline the tasks of various subsystems that will play an important role in realizing a modern communications system that transcends national boundaries. The individual systems to which I will refer here should of course be incorporated as system components in the overall composition of modern communications shown in figures 9.5 and 9.6.

Satellite Communications Systems

Through satellite communications high-quality transmission can be conducted to vast regions regardless of terrestrial distance and natural obstacles, and expenses for constructing and maintaining conventional communications routes are eliminated. Because of these features it is possible to build economically and promptly global-scale communications networks by interconnecting many geographically dispersed earth stations using the multiple access system via common satellites. Moreover, though obvious, it should be noted that this type of communications is not affected by arbitrary national boundaries.

In less than two decades satellite communications have developed as the major means of international communications, and there are currently regional satellite communications covering many countries as well as domestic satellite communications in countries with vast territory. Because of the wide bandwidth available, satellite relay of TV signals has become the indispensable means of communication for daily news services, and this has greatly contributed to mutual understanding at the grass roots level in each country. The capability of easily setting up circuits even for mobile earth stations within the beam coverage of satellites is an important feature. The maritime satellite communications system for ships is the most effective example of this application. There are usually many demands for quickly establishing satellite communications circuits in order to broadcast special events such as internationally important conferences and athletic events. The NEC Corporation has participated in and contributed to several such plans since the Tokyo Olympic Games held in 1964.

Even at present, when the world's telecommunications structure is about to shift from conventional communications to largely modern communications, the diffusion of telephones, which are closely related to economic development, is biased to some regions, and the means of information transfer are still undeveloped in more than 80 percent of the inhabited areas of the world. It may be easily imagined that if the world shifts to the modern communications age under present patterns, regional economic disparities will be aggravated, and various social conflicts may occur in many parts of the world.

Because of this situation the Independent Commission for World-Wide Telecommunications Development was established, and the members of the Commission have studied various measures to alleviate regional discrepancies in information transfer from an international perspective. I have participated in the Commission as a representative of Japan.

Satellite communications systems, with their aforementioned features, are the one medium able to introduce modern communications directly to scarcely populated regions and thus able to contribute greatly to the development of undeveloped regions. Satellite communications now being used in scarcely populated regions in Alaska, India, and Australia are the only means of information transfer and are helping to improve services in education and medical treatment.

As can be presumed from figures 9.5, 9.6, and 9.7, satellite communications will soon be widely used for high-speed data transmission, connecting various information service centers. Eventually the formation of the global databases via satellite circuits can be expected. There are various possible usage patterns, depending on the development of C&C technologies.

On the other hand, as space technology, represented by the space shuttle, progresses, it is expected that future satellites will become increasingly larger and multipurposed. The function of communications satellites will expand from conventional simple relay to regenerated relay, and further to satellites with onboard switching equipment.

For the effective use of the radio wave spectrum, the frequencies used for communicating between the ground and satellites have gradually become higher, and the 20/30 gigaHertz band will soon be widely used. At the same time effective use of frequency by space division using spot beams will be further promoted. The introduction of intersatellite links using light and millimeter waves will gradually make possible integrated satellite communications networks on a global scale.

The adoption of larger satellites and spot beams will enable simple and inexpensive earth stations to provide a variety of sophisticated services. Satellite communications will be easily applied to information transfer between offices, as well as small moving vehicles such as small ships and automobiles, not to mention direct reception of TV which is now being put into use. Thus satellite communications will play a pivotal role in realizing the dream of communications: to be able to exchange and use information on an individual, face-to-face, level without restrictions at any time or place.

TV Broadcasting Systems

On the receiving side, TV broadcasting is divided into wireless and wired systems. I would like to discuss here the demands on and possibilities for these systems, focusing on mass media by radio wave propagation which is the original function of broadcasting.

Need for Upgrading TV Broadcasting

TV broadcasting systems are used in many countries today. The basic requirements for TV broadcasting, namely instantaneity and recordability, are considered to have reached a satisfactory state. With these basic needs fulfilled, the field is now turning to higher needs. At present it appears that the future development in TV broadcasting will center on three goals as shown in figure 11.1: expanding service area, increasing volume of information, and improving broadcast quality.

Approaches to Meeting New Goals

Attempts at expanding TV broadcasting began in the 1970s. Measures were taken to set up microwave relay networks for terrestrial telecasting and to increase satellite earth stations. It goes without saying that the best way to expand the service area on a more global scale is by satellites. The *ATS-6*, launched in May 1974, was the first broadcast satellite to use an experimental 2.6 gigaHertz band. Later the *CTS* in 1976, the *ANIK-B*, the *BS*, and the *OTS-2* in 1978, and the *ANIK-C* in 1979 were

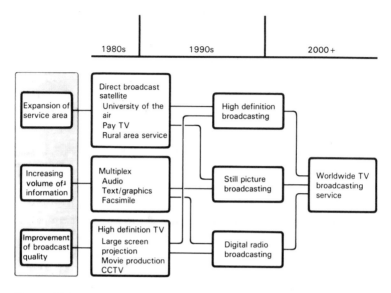

Figure 11.1
Development of TV broadcasting

launched in succession. Japan launched the *BS-2a* in 1984, with the result that the full-scale direct broadcast satellite (DBS) era is about to begin in Japan.

The United Kingdom was first to experiment with increasing the volume of information when it tried teletext broadcasting with the Ceefax field experiments conducted in 1973. Later France, West Germany, Sweden, the United States, and Canada began experimenting with the system. In Japan teletext broadcasting has reached its final stage just prior to practical application.

Concerning the need for improving quality, Japan proposed a study program on high-definition TV to CCIR in 1972, and this proposal was formally adopted in 1974. High-definition TV has been actively studied in some countries since then.

To enable the widespread use of these new broadcast media, it is necessary that all countries involved agree on unified international specifications as quickly as possible.

Possibilities of New Broadcasting Forms

When the various systems described here reach the stage of practical application, various new possibilities will open up as a result of their being used in combinations. Let me give a few examples. First, high-quality telecasting using high-definition TV taking advantage of the wide bandwidth transmission characteristics of satellites can be envisioned. Still picture broadcasting, which sends a large quantity of information using one-channel TV broadcasting, and PCM audio broadcasting, which can broadcast ten- to fifteen-channel PCM audio signals simultaneously, also come to mind. Although information is not transmitted on request, virtually all important information can be on tap twenty-four hours a day, like city water, and consumers can select and receive what they need. Further, since these broadcasts can be transmitted worldwide, they will greatly influence developing international exchanges in education, art, meteorology, living comforts, medical information, and the environment.

Information Service Center Systems

Next, I would like to consider the intelligent information service centers shown in figures 9.5 through 9.8. First come shared computation centers. Generally speaking, computer functions are heading toward lower prices, distributed processing, and use of intelligent terminals. However, the necessity for computation centers, including shared computing centers that provide high-grade scientific and technological computing using advanced super computers, will continue to exist. Beyond that lies the need for such centers to be available for international use.

The next function of information service centers is to generate systematically information as a new, varied, ever-expanding social and public resource, to store it, and then to make it available promptly and conveniently whenever the necessity arises. For this purpose it will become important to install automated international information service centers, which will necessitate the use of satellite communications systems.

As you can imagine, in the case of international information centers, multilanguage access will be necessary. To solve this problem, automatic translation technology will be required for both registration in, input into, and retrieval from the database. An international cooperative structure will also become necessary. The task here is closely related to the automatic interpretation telephone system which will be taken up in the next section.

Other key technological issues concern processing and storage. Information in the future will increasingly take on the nature of being one of humankind's shared assets. Therefore measures for large and super large computers and large capacity files, as well as measures for long-term storage and security of the information, will become extremely important.

The information service centers will play a major role as databases in the fields where the development of advanced science and technology and international information distribution are required. It will be important to build up databases in the various areas of scientific applications, particularly databases dealing with, for example, chemical structures, bioengineering, and medical information. As international information service centers, technological information databases, hygiene and welfare information databases, and food information databases will be likely candidates. The information service centers in fact will perform a vital role in promoting mutual international understanding.

Automatic Interpretation Telephone Systems

At present people can talk between the major cities of the world at any time by directly dialing the number of the other party. However, such a development in international communications capabilities has yet to produce sufficiently mutual understanding among nations in today's world. One of the major obstacles is the difference in languages from nation to nation.

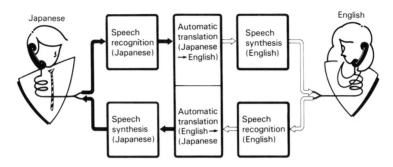

Figure 11.2
Automatic interpretation telephone system

In order to overcome this problem, it was once considered that a common world language, such as Esperanto, be adopted. However, despite the efforts of people promoting Esperanto, it has not caught on. The language of any people is inseparable from its culture, and we have to see that it is respected to the fullest extent in the future as in the past.

Accordingly I think that the development of an automatic interpretation telephone system as a component in global modern communications is a promising means of solving this problem. As described in chapter 3, the NEC Corporation has an advanced speech recognition and synthesis technology that has been developed over the past twenty-odd years. Eventually, by integrating sentence analysis/translation processing technology with this, if the other party speaks to me in English, I will be able to hear it in Japanese, and vice versa, my thoughts expressed in Japanese will be translated into English and conveyed to the other party. It is my dream to realize such a system. Figure 11.2 shows how the system will work.

Before this automatic interpretation telephone system can become a reality, further development is required in both the software technology, which clarifies required processing algorithms and forms a unified large-scale processing system, and the hardware technology, which realizes the high-speed processing system executing the large-scale software on a real-time basis.

As for the software, the technology for voice recognition and synthesis of a limited number of words has already been developed and put into practical use. In place of this we now need to develop the recognition and synthesis technology for an unlimited vocabulary. This is extremely challenging and will require a major technical breakthrough. Moreover, to achieve the recognition and synthesis of arbitrary speech, the difficult work of preparing a lexicon and grammatical processing rules for each language is indispensable.

In the sentence analysis/translation processing technology, it is necessary to upgrade and generalize the machine translation technology that is now beginning to be put into practical use. Furthermore, in order to make translations among many languages possible, processing systems devoted to each language must be developed.

The common technology required for developing such software includes so-called nonnumerical processing technologies such as symbolic processing, inference processing, and knowledge-based processing. These types of technologies will play a central role in the next generation of computer systems. They are being developed in the Japanese Fifth Generation Computer Development Project, a ten-year plan initiated in fiscal 1982.

With respect to hardware, it is important to develop architecture that can execute efficiently large-scale nonnumerical processing software, and likewise, it is important to upgrade the device technology that will make it possible, namely LSI technology.

In high-level processing such as automatic interpretation, the processing equipment required will be close to that of the human brain in complexity. In the field of semiconductor integrated circuit technology, fine-pattern processing technology is steadily progressing as an extension of conventional technology. As you know, the degree of integration and the processing speed are increasing every year. Recently, in place of conventional integration on a two-dimensional plane, three-dimensional IC technology constituting cubic circuits has begun to be developed. By means of such breakthroughs, it is expected that the VLSI will continue to move progressively to higher integration and performance in the future.

When such an automatic interpretation telephone system is realized, how will it be integrated into the modern communications system shown in figures 9.5 through 9.8? Because the automatic interpretation telephone system will be comparatively large and expensive in the beginning, it will be installed at a centralized information service center near an international gateway station and will be shared by many people. However, with reductions in size and price, it will gradually be used beside terminals and will be installed as part of office processing equipment. Eventually it might even be incorporated into telephone sets.

For the development of this automatic interpretation telephone, international cooperation is not only welcome but expected. International cooperation is particularly necessary for the development of the processing algorithms for each language in speech recognition and synthesis and sentence analysis processing.

Teleconferencing Systems

To improve business efficiency in offices, some measures may be taken in the area of conferences or meetings. In organizations where the offices of the conference participants are geographically dispersed, teleconferencing at two or more locations can be an very effective. Even in small organizations where people are located in one building, the intelligent conference room facilities should be a good way of improving business efficiency, for example, by automatically recording proceedings. This is considered the most basic form of (tele)conferencing.

Nevertheless, the teleconferencing system is an important constituent element of the wide area office automation system.

By sharing or connecting with facilities in the normal office automation system, this is where the future development toward C&C is expected to be greatest.

Figure 11.3 shows the conceptual outline of the teleconferencing system. The functions required for teleconferencing systems are arranged in developmental stages as follows:

First stage   Communications functions utilizing media such as voice, data, and graphics.

Second stage   Information retrieval and simulation functions interfacing with related information communications systems.

Third stage   Conference material preparation, recording, editing, and reporting functions using an information processing and storage systems.

Fourth stage   Automatic translation functions for international teleconferencing.

Particularly concerning global international meetings for which participants must otherwise spend long hours traveling long distances, the use of international teleconferencing is a very attractive alternative. In building such international teleconferencing systems, the tasks to be considered are as follows:

• *Development of technology for efficient transmission of wide bandwidth information such as pictures*   Since in teleconferencing many terminals use wide bandwidth transmission lines simultaneously for long periods of time, efficient use of transmission lines is important.

• *Development of efficient system conversion technology for different TV standards, and the standardization of various protocols.*

• *Development of automatic interpretation and translation technologies*   In teleconferencing there are cases where one language has to be interpreted simultaneously into several languages, as described in the previous section. In addition to automatic interpretation, it would be necessary to translate the materials to be presented at the conference.

• *Resolution of time zone factors*   Fundamental resolution of the matter of time differences is very difficult. However, it may

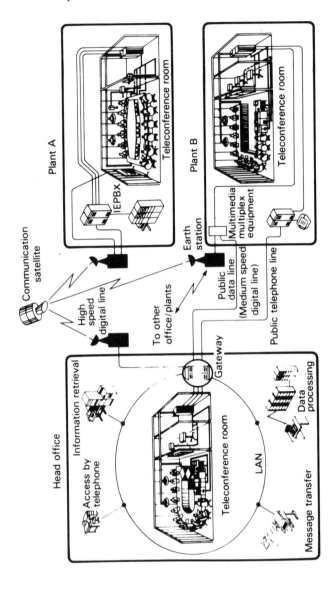

Figure 11.3
Teleconferencing systems

be possible to alleviate the problems caused by time differences in real-time teleconferencing by utilizing audio, video, and recording and processing technologies for conference materials prior to the actual communications. Well-prepared nonreal-time computer conferencing could become another good countermeasure to this situation.

12

Promotion of International Cooperation and Exchange

In the preceding chapter, as a first strategy I advocated positioning modern communications systems as a global infrastructure. As a second strategy concerning modern communications, I suggest that international cooperation and exchange be strongly promoted.

International Shared Use of Satellites

Communications Satellites

INTELSAT was established by a resolution of the United Nations General Assembly that aimed at a global satellite communications system to enable all people on earth to communicate from any one country to another without restrictions. INTELSAT started international commercial communications in May 1965 in the Atlantic Ocean region with the geostationary satellite, *INTELSAT I* (nicknamed *Early Bird*). Succeedingly three *INTELSAT III* satellites were launched in 1968, covering the Atlantic, Indian, and Pacific oceans. These satellites, which cover the entire world, formed the first step in establishing a reliable worldwide satellite communications network.

The remarkable development of the INTELSAT system has splendidly embodied the hopes placed on outer space by humankind. As an international cooperative effort it is also a product of the wisdom of humankind. The process of its development

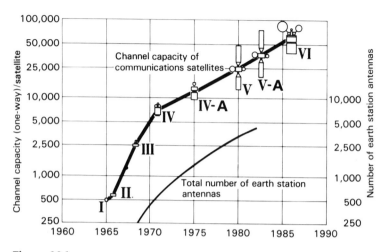

Figure 12.1
Development of the INTELSAT system

and future prospects are shown in figure 12.1, demonstrating its potential for truly impressive growth.

In addition to international communications, INTELSAT opened the way for domestic communications. Lease services for transponders located in the satellites were started in 1975, and twenty countries now use the service. In order to respond to new worldwide demands for satellite communications, applications to comparatively economical communication services such as business communications, teleconferencing, and thinroute services are planned. All are based on international cooperation and shared use.

The INMARSAT system, a kind of mobile communications system such as was mentioned in chapter 10, was established by the International Maritime Satellite Organization (IMCO) of the United Nations in July 1979. It succeeded the MARISAT system services initiated by the United States and began operations in February 1981. This service started an immediate-trend in maritime communications away from the relatively

Table 12.1 Installation status of INMARSAT stations

	Coastal earth stations	Ship stations
End of 1981	3	1,000
End of 1982	6	1,500
End of 1984	13	3,000
End of 1980s		8,000 or more

unstable, low-quality medium- and shortwave communications that had been used for many years toward highly reliable high-quality satellite communications. It has made it possible for ships, irrespective of their nationality, to communicate from any offshore area of the world. As shown in table 12.1, IN-MARSAT will continue to develop rapidly by making the most of its coverage of vast sea areas with high quality communications through the cooperation of the major countries of the world.

In the future INMARSAT is reportedly aiming at small-antenna applications for small ships and sea rescue, the collection and dissemination of meteorological observation data from and to ships, and data link services with civil aircraft under joint studies with related United Nations agencies. Thus new fields of international shared use will be expanded even further.

In addition to the satellites already mentioned, there are the Indonesian Palapa satellites already in use by ASEAN countries, the European ESC, and the ARABSAT regional satellites. These are clear examples of the expanding, international shared use of satellites. Such satellites will not only promote international friendship but also bring about immeasurable economic, cultural, and educational benefits. This trend is also quite desirable from the standpoint of the internationally effective use of geostationary orbits and the frequency spectrum.

Meteorological Observation Satellites

Japan's geostationary meteorological satellite *Himawari* is a typical example of international cooperation concerning satellites. It was launched to help implement the world meteorological observation plan passed by the United Nations World Meteorological Organization in 1963, in which five geostationary satellites and two polar orbit satellites were proposed to carry out global meteorological observations in an international project. This plan has already been realized on a worldwide scale.

The meteorological satellites developed by NASA in the United States, ESA in Europe, and NASDA in Japan are now widely used on an international basis. The meteorological information gathered by these satellites is not only sent around the globe to aviation and marine users but also has become a part of daily life in the form of weather forecasts on TV and in newspapers. The information is also widely used for the study of long-term worldwide meteorological changes and the prediction of the courses of typhoons or hurricanes. The meteorological information from *Himawari* launched by Japan is utilized by fifteen countries in Oceania and Asia, including Australia, Singapore, Thailand, the Philippines, China, and Korea.

The uses of artificial satellites are not limited to those described thus far. Their utilization will increase in many areas, such as in surveying of natural resources of outer space, exploration of planets, and development of space laboratories and factories. They are promoting closer international cooperation on the usefulness of space whose infinite reaches have for many years provided humankind with fantastic futuristic dreams. The realization of such dreams will clearly demand unceasing worldwide cooperation.

Tasks of International Information Flow

The development of communications technologies progressively reduces the transfer cost of information. In conventional communications the cost of communications is relatively higher than the value of the information. In this situation the circulation of information can be considered to have been suppressed at a relatively high economic equilibrium point.

As the value of information rises progressively and the cost of information circulation falls, the economic equilibrium point will come down to a level where enormous quantities of information can flow. The so-called information society is nothing but a society that has reached this point. The advances of C&C technology ensure the coming of such a society, and we now stand in a transition period leading to the information society era.

Once this era is established, information itself will tend to flow in great volume, making the existing economic and social structures, as well as the legal systems of individual countries irrelevant. Information is basically and essentially something that should be known and shared by many people, and it is only the level of technology that has so far suppressed it. The development of C&C technology will release humankind from today's technical constraints.

Because existing social structures are not fully prepared for unrestricted circulation of massive amounts of information, contradictions and imbalances of various types will arise. Among them, the greatest and most serious problem is that of transborder data flow (TBDF) in which information crosses national boundaries. The massive transborder flow of information related to commercial transactions will entirely change the concept of the conventional physical trade of commodities. The mechanisms that nations have constructed to date to maintain their borders may not be applicable in their present form. It is this problem that is now actively being discussed in many international organizations (such as UNESCO, UNCTC, OECD, and IBI) and international private agencies (such as ICC, INTUG, and BIAC).

This is one of the important social tasks that the development of C&C technology has brought forth. I will not go any more extensively into this TBDF problem here, but I would like to point out that it should be recognized that the unrestricted flow of information will be a key factor in promoting business activities in the future and that it will improve the efficiency of corporate management and raise productivity. Moreover the unrestricted circulation of information domestically and internationally will promote the industries of communications equipment, information equipment, software, information services, VANs, and relevant kinds of information that cover various information systems or OA systems in offices. These will become the new basic industries stimulating the world economy. Therefore laws restricting transborder data flow should be minimized. The remaining restrictions should be based on the maintenance of harmonious order, security, and integrity—which are principles all people can support.

I believe the development of C&C technology will not stop at the scope described here. It will inspire the boundless wisdom of humankind to make unlimited progress. But regulations for new information communications should be flexible. They should prompt fair competition among different enterprises in order to promote innovations and thus lead the international information society to prosperity. What is more, regulations must be always reviewed as advances in technology. For solving the problems related to regulations, it may be especially desirable to establish a forum where all relevant points can be thoroughly discussed and an international consensus obtained.

I have described modern communications particularly from the standpoint of communications as one aspect of the overall functions of C&C—the integration of computers and communications—and I have discussed the various programs for its strategic development.

I have taken up modern communications systems as systems that combine computer functions in a broad sense (namely functions to assist electronically human beings in information processing and storage) with conventional communications (namely information transfer) where varieties of information media at the human interface are taken into scope in a well-balanced way.

I have presented an overall picture of modern communications systems as social infrastructures to be integrated globally across national boundaries. At the user level, terminals handling numerous information with various human interfaces and varied information service centers will be connected by a variety of transparent communications networks.

I have examined the multilayered structure of communications networks centering on transparent communications networks, home communications services, LAN and WAN in business communications, mobile communications, VAN, and new electronic media, which are part of my overall vision of modern communications.

Finally, I have indicated the importance of tasks aimed at developing systems for international modern communications, including international satellite communications systems. I have considered some tasks of international cooperation and exchange that are not only useful but also necessary for building modern communications systems.

As you can guess from the foregoing discussion, advances in microelectronics, optoelectronics, and computer technologies in both hardware and software are about to change thoroughly the today's concept of communications. The influences modern communications will exert on culture, civilization, industry, and economies will exceed by far the developments brought about by conventional telecommunications during the past century.

Conclusion

I have tried to position and introduce C&C so that the reader will come to understand that this concept did not emanate from a simple sudden idea or whim. Rather, I reached the concept of C&C through several continuing, well-grounded processes deriving from the historical background of NEC and my own experience of fifty-six years since joining the company.

I particularly feel this direction was a natural outcome of judgments and decisions I made early in my twenty-one-year tenure as chief executive officer of NEC, which I always aimed at the ongoing growth and development of the company. One of my most important decisions was to establish priority investment in the semiconductor business some twenty years ago when I considered the possibility of developing a "knowledge industry."

As I observed the remarkable progress of semiconductor devices—starting with transistors, and progressing to ICs, LSIs, and VLSIs—I predicted that epoch-making changes would be brought to the communications and computer fields if both were based on these semiconductor devices. And as I anticipated, digitalization progressed rapidly to communications technology.

I understood too that since computers were originally based on digital technology, digitalization of communications would cause communications and computer technologies to become homogeneous. As one manifestation of this, the trend in the computer field has been away from dependence on centralized large-scale computers to distributed processing systems that provide functions equivalent to or even greater than those of large-scale computers by connecting a number of small- or medium-scale computers through communications networks.

As digitalization progressed in the communications field, effective use of computer technology gradually came to be seen in the transmission, reception, and switching of information. Based on this trend, I foresaw the necessity of computer and communications technologies eventually merging. Thus I reached the concept of C&C—the integration of computers and communications—which I made NEC's corporate identity.

As we entered the 1980s, new and important progress was being made in the concept of C&C, but attention was paid only to the technical factors on which it was mainly formed, not the human factors inherent in the concept of C&C. By this I mean, it is humans who develop the C&C system, and likewise, it is humans who utilize the information provided by the C&C system.

Therefore I proposed a new expression "Man and C&C," which has brought a third dimension to the integration of computers and communications—an axis representing human beings. Clearly from the beginning of the development of computers and communications, the full performance of machines was obtained only after humans learned how to use them, which often required great effort. Although remarkable progress in C&C systems has been made, advanced systems still require great effort on the part of humans to derive their full performance potential.

My ideal is for anyone, not just experts, to use C&C systems easily and thus to achieve a more satisfying cultural, economic, and social life. Machines are machines and are therefore subservient to humans. I believe that the humans will never lose their superiority in activities requiring intelligence.

The areas that depend on human effort are centered on software. Software is required for activating and applying C&C systems. As we look at the present software situation, we see that it is coming under serious strain due to the remarkable and rapid increase in the demand for new applications. In fact today we have entered an age of software crisis.

According to calculations by an American scholar, if the situation is allowed to continue, the number of people required to develop and upgrade software will surpass the world's total population by the year 2025! This indicates that if things proceed as they do now, today's problems will never be resolved. It may be no exaggeration to say that C&C's usefulness to humankind depends on a successful assessment of software production.

I think also that in order for C&C systems to be utilized effectively, it is indispensable that we develop appropriate software to meet differences in languages and life-styles. Even if the same hardware is used, different application software will be necessary, depending on the countries or situations in which C&C is used.

Because of this I believe that it will become necessary for each country to be able to produce its own software in order to build C&C systems rooted in and suitable for its economic and social structures, as well as its historical and cultural background. Another reason why this is desirable in software is the matter of expense required for development.

Software expenses include not only those for actual development but also those for adding or changing functions during the life of the software, which are called maintenance expenses. These maintenance expenses carry great weight.

Maintenance expenses can be quite formidable, indeed—the cost of maintenance often is twice that of development. Moreover the extent of additions or changes may vary enormously—at one extreme, requiring advanced and innovative technologies, and at the other, perfunctory servicing that can be handled by comparatively less skilled engineers. In introducing and operating C&C systems, it will be fully possible for people of each country to add or change software to meet their operating requirements, and it will be desirable for them to do so.

A clearer picture of C&C's future contribution to the general public can be made by viewing it from an entirely new perspective as a multilayered structure of communications networks. The different C&C applications then are classified by the character of each market. The structure has three layers comprising public, business, and home applications. I first presented this concept publicly in 1982 at a special address before the general meeting of the alumni association of the Massachusetts Institute of Technology [6].

In modern communications, development is anticipated in various ways in each of these three markets. First, among the public services available through C&C are the basic communications networks of each country, which are part of the country's national infrastructure. I believe these can be connected to global networks to form broader infrastructures for communications. Among other developments, new communications satellite systems, submarine optical fiber cable systems, TV broadcasting systems, and information service center systems represent means to actualize these global networks.

Next, in businesses we can expect new developments in both local area networks (LAN) and wide area networks (WAN). In relation to these, I believe advances will be made in office automation and factory automation equipment.

Finally, in home applications I greatly anticipate a wider variety of products and services, which are collectively known as new electronic media.

Among all these crowning achievements of modern communications, I would like to highlight what has long been a dream of mine: the automatic interpretation telephone system. Throughout my fifty-six-year career at NEC, I have made it my mission to help create a situation that would make it possible for any person in the world to communicate with any other person at any place and any time. I believe that one of the major reasons for the lack of mutual understanding between various countries and cultures is language—the fact that people of different countries cannot talk to each other, or the number of people who can talk freely with people of other countries is extremely limited. With the automatic interpretation telephone this barrier can be completely removed, and people will be able to communicate naturally in their own language with anyone in the world who has access to a telephone. In other words, the average person who is not fluent in a foreign language will be able to converse with individuals of other countries. This situation may raise the level of international communication and help eliminate misunderstandings among nations that might lead to conflicts or struggles. Communication at the grass-roots level is the most powerful tool for deepening mutual understanding among nations.

It may be that with language barriers removed the people of the world will overcome feelings of being separate races enclosed by national boundaries and will realize that they are members of the same great family of humankind. The sharing of this feeling may greatly contribute to true world peace among nations of this planet. Thus the automatic interpretation telephone system may help realize world peace in a significant way.

At present the technology for machines that translate text is quite advanced, and basic models have already been commercialized. However, an automatic interpretation system is an entirely different story. By "interpretation" I mean to take a spoken conversation in one language and convert it instantaneously into another language in a form understandable to the listener. To achieve this, the machine must have automatic speech recognition and synthesis technologies as well as technologies for automatically analyzing and processing interpretation of spoken sentences. On top of that, the machine will have to work on an on-line, real-time basis. In short, the machine will require the integration and concentration of highly intelligent processing technologies. I consider this to be one of the ultimate forms of Man and C&C.

I think that the development of automatic interpretation telephone systems will serve as an effective index for the progress of C&C. In 1983, at the TELCOM 83 exhibition in Geneva, NEC demonstrated a research model that could provide rudimentary interpretation between English and Japanese, and English and Spanish. This demonstration greatly impressed those who saw it.

In my experience I have seen that it takes about twenty years of effort from the conception of an epoch-making technology to its realization. The digital PCM system, the geostationary communications satellite, and optical communications technology have all been such cases. This automatic interpretation telephone system may not be an exception. However, I anticipate that it will be completed before the year 2000. Despite my advanced age I am still pushing for its achievement in the hope that this might be the greatest gift to humankind from C&C.

Since my presentation some eight years ago of the concept of C&C at INTELCOM 77, in Atlanta, I have presented a paper elaborating the Man and C&C concept. I have also seen the number of people throughout the world who share this concept growing. An American scholar has advocated a new word, "compunications," which, although a little different in expression, shares common ground with C&C in that it is based on the idea of the merging of computers and communications. Interestingly too AT&T, the world's largest communications company, is moving into the computer field, and IBM, the giant in the computer world, is moving into the communications field. I believe that C&C will constitute the central trend in electronics in the late 1980s, and I am confident that this trend will continue into the twenty-first century.

Thus I would like to offer this book to the world, wishing that the concept of C&C will eventually bring happiness and prosperity to all humankind by transcending artificial boundaries on earth and reducing the language barriers between peoples. A global society transcending national borders must be developed. I hope that the concept of C&C will contribute greatly to the development of the knowledge and information society I envision in the twenty-first century.

References

1. K. Kobayashi. 1977. "Shaping a Communications Industry to Meet the Ever-Changing Needs of Society." INTELCOM '77, Atlanta, Georgia, October.

2. K. Kobayashi. 1978. "The Japanese Computer Industry: Its Roots and Development." 3rd U.S.-Japan Computer Conference at San Francisco, Calif., Cosponsored by AFIPS and IPSJ, October.

3. K. Kobayashi. 1981. "Computers, Communications and Man: the Integration of Computers and Communications with Man as an Axis—The Role of Software." 23rd IEEE Computer Society International Conference at Washington, D.C., September 16.

4. K. Kobayashi. 1982. "Man and 'C&C': Concept and Perspectives." International Institute of Communications Annual Conference, Helsinki, Finland, September 6.

5. K. Kobayashi. 1983. "Strategic Approaches to Modern Communications: 'C&C.' " ITU 4th World Telecommunication Forum, Geneva, Switzerland, October 27.

6. K. Kobayashi. 1982. "Future Role of 'C&C' in the Home." 1982 General Meeting of MIT Alumni Association, Cambridge, Mass., June 11.

7. A. Nakashima. 1935. "A Construction Theory for Relay Circuits." *Journal of the Institute of Telegraph and Telephone Engineers*, September (in Japanese). A. Nakashima and M. Hanzawa. 1936. "Algebraic Expressions Relative to Simple Partial Path in Relay Circuits (No. 1)." *Journal of the Institute of Telegraph and Telephone Engineers*, December (in Japanese). A. Nakashima and M. Hanzawa. 1937. "Algebraic Expressions Relative to Simple Partial Path in Relay Circuits (No. 2)." *Journal of the Institute of Telegraph and Telephone Engineers*, February (in Japanese). A. Nakashima. 1970. "Memory of the Theory on Switching Circuit Networks." *Journal of Electronics and Communication Engineers of Japan*, December (in Japanese).

8. C. E. Shannon. 1938. "Algebraic Analysis of Relay and Switching Circuits." *Transactions of AIEE* 57.

9. H. Takahashi. 1972. "The Birth of Electronic Computers," *Chukoshinsho*, no. 273, p. 20.

10. M. Morita and S. Ito. 1960. "High Sensitivity Receiving System for Frequency Modulated Wave." IRE International Convention, March.

11. H. Watanabe. 1957. "Synthesis of Band-pass LADDER Networks." *Journal of the Institute of Electrical Communication Engineers of Japan*, October (in Japanese). H. Watanabe. 1958. "Synthesis of Band-pass LADDER Network." *Transactions on Circuit Theory of IRE*, CT Vol. CT-5 No. 4., December. H. Watanabe. 1960. "Approximation Theory of Filter Networks." *Journal of the Institute of Electrical Communication Engineers of Japan*, March (in Japanese). H. Watanabe. 1961. "Approximation Theory for Filter Networks." *Transactions on Circuit Theory of IRE*, CT Vol. CT-9 No. 3., September.

12. H. Sakoe and S. Chiba. 1978. "Dynamic Programming Algorithm Optimization for Spoken Word Recognition." *IEEE Transactions on Acoustics, Speech, Signal Processing*, Vol. ASSP-26 No. 1, February. H. Sakoe. 1979. "Two-Level DP-Matching—A Dynamic Programming-Based Pattern Matching Algorithm for Connected Word Recognition." *IEEE Transactions of ASSP*, Vol. ASSP-27, No. 6, December.

13. K. Kobayashi. 1982. "NEC's Management and Its 'C&C' Strategy." Graduate School of Business Administration, Harvard University, Boston, Mass., December.

14. K. Kobayashi. 1966. Text of Special Address at the National Joint Convention of the Four Major Electrical Institutes of Japan, April 1966 (in Japanese).

15. A. Gupta, and H. D. Toong. 1984. "Insights into Personal Computers." chapter 17; K. Kobayashi, K. Watanabe, R. Ichikawa, and A. Kato. 1984. "The Personal Computer in 'C&C.' " Proceedings of the IEEE, March.

16. K. Kobayashi. 1980. *C&C Is the Wisdom of Japan*, The Simul Press, Tokyo, Japan.

17. K. Kobayashi. 1982. *C&C and Software*, The Simul Press, Tokyo, Japan.

Supplementary Bibliography

Honda, K., and Saito, S. 1920. "On K.S. Magnet Steel." *Journal of Institute of Electrical Engineers of Japan* 40.

Kato, Y., and Takei, T. 1933. "Permanent Oxide Magnet and Its Characteristics." *Journal of Institute of Electrical Engineers of Japan* 53 (May).

Koga, I., and Shoyama, M. 1936. "Notes on Piezoelectric Quartz Crystals." Proceedings of Institute of Radio Engineers 24 (March).

Kurokawa, H., Someya, I., and Morita, M. 1957. "New Microwave Repeater System Using a Single Traveling-Wave Tube as Both Amplifier and Local Oscillator." Proceedings of Institute of Radio Engineers 45 (December).

Masumoto, H., and Yamamoto, T. 1937. "On Magnetic and Electric Characteristics of the New Alloy 'SENDUST' and Fe-Si-Al Alloy." *Journal of the Japan Institute of Metal* 1 (March).

Mishima, T. 1953. "On Characteristics of MT Magnetic Steel." *Journal of Institute of Electrical Engineers of Japan* 73 (October).

Matsumae, S., Shinohara, N., and Hashimoto, G. 1932. "A Proposal to Introduce Non-Loaded Cables for Long-Distance Telephone Circuits." *Journal of Institute of Telegraph and Telephone Engineers of Japan* (May).

Matsumae, S., Yonezawa, S., and Kurokawa, K. 1939. "The Multiplex Carrier Telephony on Ultra-Shortwave at Strait of Tsugaru." *Journal of Institute of Electrical Engineers of Japan* 59.

Matsushiro, M. 1898. "Marconi System Radio Telegraphy." *Journal of Institute of Electrical Engineers of Japan* 18 (July).

Metzger, S., and Sekimoto, T. 1974. "SPADE System." *Journal of Institute of Electrical Communication Engineers of Japan* 57 (August).

Morita, M., et al. 1966. "STAR System." NEC Research and Development. (October).

Nagai, K., Igarashi, T., and Ishikawa, M. 1940. "A Magnetic Recording System Using A.C. Bias Method." Japanese Patent No. 136997. Applied in 1938. Registered in June 1940.

Niwa, Y., and Kobayashi, M. 1929. "One System of Electrical Transmission of Pictures." *Journal of Institute of Electrical Engineers of Japan* 49 (February).

Nukiyama, H., and Matsudaira, M. 1927. "The Vibrometer." *Journal of Institute of Electrical Engineers of Japan* 47 (May).

Okabe, K. 1928. "Production of Intense Extra-Short Electromagnetic Waves by 'Split Anode Magnetron.' " *Journal of Institute of Electrical Engineers of Japan* 48 (March).

Shimazu, Y. 1929. "A System of Supervisory Control." Proceedings of the World Engineering Congress at Tokyo, Japan (July).

Takayanagi, K. 1928. "Experiments on Television." *Journal of Institute of Electrical Engineers of Japan* 48 (September).

Torikata, U. 1914. "T-Y-K System of Radio Telegraphy and Radio Telephony." *Journal of Institute of Electrical Engineers of Japan.* Lecture (October).

Uda, S. 1929. "Wireless Telephony on Extremely Short Wave." *Journal of Institute of Electrical Engineers of Japan* 49 (October).

Watanabe, Y. 1949. "Some Remarks on the Equation of Thermionic Emission." Technology Reports of Tohoku University 14 (September).

Watanabe, Y., Kasahara, H., and Nakamura, Y. 1938. "A-Type Sendytron Using a New Method of Starting an Arc." *Electrotechnical Journal of Japan* 2 (August).

Yagi, H., and Uda, S. 1926. "Projector of the Sharpest Beam of the Electric Waves." Proceedings of Imperial Academy of Japan. No. 2.

Yonezawa, S., and Tanaka, N. 1963. "Microwave Communication." Maruzen Co. Ltd. Tokyo, Japan.